JUN 19 2007

Invasive Terrestrial Plants

INVASIVE SPECIES

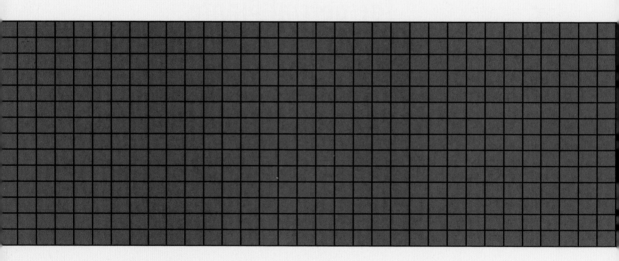

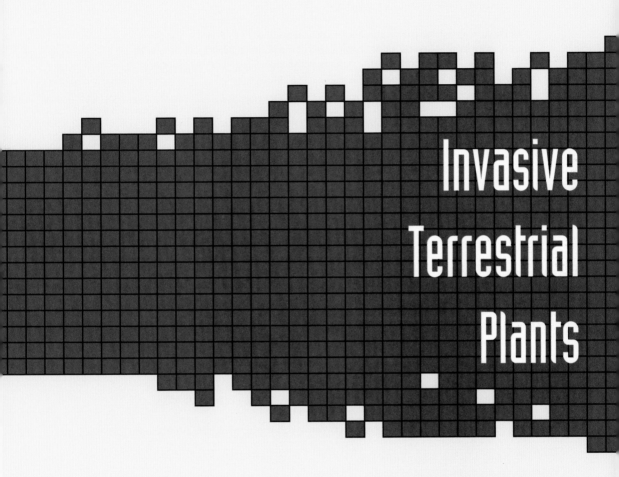

INVASIVE SPECIES

Invasive Terrestrial Plants

Suellen May

CHELSEA HOUSE
PUBLISHERS
An imprint of Infobase Publishing

Invasive Terrestrial Plants

Chelsea House
An imprint of Infobase Publishing
132 West 31st Street
New York NY 10001

Library of Congress Cataloging-in-Publication Data

May, Suellen.
 Invasive terrestrial plants / Suellen May.
    p. cm. — (Invasive species)
 Includes bibliographical references and index.
 ISBN 0-7910-9128-7 (hardcover)
 1. Invasive plants—Juvenile literature. 2. Noxious weeds—Juvenile literature.
 I. Title. II. Series: May, Suellen. Invasive species
  SB613.5.M39 2006
  581.7'18--dc22

                                    2006009058

Chelsea House books are available at special discounts when purchased in bulk quantities for businesses, associations, institutions, or sales promotions. Please call our Special Sales Department in New York at (212) 967-8800 or (800) 322-8755.

You can find Chelsea House on the World Wide Web at http://www.chelseahouse.com

Text design by James Scotto-Lavino
Cover design by Takeshi Takahashi

Printed in the United States of America

Bang JSL 10 9 8 7 6 5 4 3 2 1

This book is printed on acid-free paper.

All links and Web addresses were checked and verified to be correct at the time of publication. Because of the dynamic nature of the Web, some addresses and links may have changed since publication and may no longer be valid.

TABLE OF CONTENTS

The Natural World of Terrestrial Plants

Terrestrial or land plants use sunlight, carbon dioxide, and water to make food. Plants have mineral requirements, just like animals, to maintain their tissues and cells. For **terrestrial plants**, these nutrients come from the soil. Terrestrial plants can be either woody or herbaceous. An example of a woody plant is a tree. Grasses and other plants with nonwoody stems are herbaceous plants. Terrestrial plants get their nutrients primarily from root absorption in the soil. Aquatic or wetland plants get their nutrients from root absorption in wetlands, oceans, rivers, or streams.

Terrestrial plants play an important role in an ecosystem by providing food and shelter for wildlife. A common shrub found in Western states, four-winged saltbush (*Atriplex canescens*) produces seeds that are eaten by birds, provides cover for deer and other small mammals, and is a host for larval butterflies. Many trees produce berries that are eaten by birds; beavers eat the bark of some trees; and flowers provide nectar for birds and insects. Deer also browse on the twigs of shrubs and trees of shorter stature. Without plants, insects and animals, including people, would not survive.

NATIVE TERRESTRIAL PLANTS

Native terrestrial plants occur naturally in a particular region, state, ecosystem, and habitat without direct or indirect human actions. Some scientists think of native as a plant that is from a specific country or region within a country; others think of it more strictly as within a specific ecosystem. A plant that is native to the grasslands of Colorado would be nonnative in a Pennsylvania hardwood forest.

Native terrestrial plants have evolved with their environment. Terrestrial plants native to a specific area will flower and set seed at an appropriate time given the climate.

Terrestrial plants brought from other states' nurseries or through other means would not be considered native to the state it was brought. Native plants exist and interact with native insects. The insects are the plants' predators. Predators and prey are part of nature's balance and help prevent plant populations from growing out of control.

NONNATIVE TERRESTRIAL PLANTS

Nonnative or exotic terrestrial plants are from a foreign ecosystem. They were accidentally or intentionally relocated. Hundreds of years ago people did not realize the potential problems of bringing terrestrial plants from other countries. And in many cases, there were endless benefits to importing nonnatives, such as valuable crops like corn. Immigrants coming to the United States brought terrestrial plants and seeds from their countries as a way to remember their former homes. Many of the nonnative terrestrial plants that now grow in the United States are from Europe and Asia because that is where so many Americans are from.

The problem with nonnative terrestrial plants is that they are generally introduced without their natural predators. In their native country, these terrestrial plants have insects and pathogens (disease-causing organisms) to keep their populations under control. Insects and pathogens control a plant's population by injuring the plant and causing stress and disease and eventually death.

Insects specifically control plants by nature's predator-prey relationship. The presence of both insect and plant prevents one or the other's population from growing out of control. An increase in the plant population results in a larger food supply for the insect. Insect populations rise due to the increase in food.

Do Plants Native to the United States Become Invasive in Other Countries?

Yes, it's true. Plants from the United States are guilty of invading and disturbing ecosystems abroad. These invaders are introduced in the same ways that invasive plants have been introduced in the United States, either accidentally or intentionally.

The native box elder tree (*Acer negundo*) is a good example. This deciduous tree is native to North America and was introduced to Australia as an ornamental. In Australia, this fast-growing tree invades bushland, particularly along waterways or streams. Although kept in balance in North America because of the presence of natural predators, box elder has no predators in Australia. This is the reason it can grow rapidly and invade precious habitat in Australia. The box elder's invasion changes the landscape of Australia and displaces native trees and shrubs.

Another species native to North America but invasive in Australia is black willow (*Salix nigra*). Black willow is kept in perfect balance in terms of its population along waterways in North America. In Australia, this plant spreads rapidly by seeds from the winged dry fruit that appears before leaves in the spring. Black willow is found mostly along the southeastern coast of Australia invading bushland and waterways.

Like the United States, Australia recognizes the problem with invasive species and has their own national weed management plan that involves prevention, identification, education, and control.

As insect populations begin to grow larger, food supplies in the form of plants dwindle, the insect population falls and gives rise to more plants, and the cycle continues. This cycle keeps either the insect or plant numbers from growing out of control.

People have caused this cycle to go out of balance by traveling across continents and introducing non native plants to lands that the plants would never travel to. Invasive plants disturb ecosystems because a foreign plant has been introduced to an environment in which it does not belong. Native animals may prefer not to eat the nonnative plants that they did not evolve with.

Many nonnatives thrive because they have characteristics that make them outstanding plant competitors. These characteristics include producing lots of seeds, growing very fast, or containing toxic or poisonous plant parts. Some plants even produce a natural herbicide from the roots that inhibits the growth of other plants.

INVASIVE TERRESTRIAL PLANTS

Invasive terrestrial plants are aggressive, highly competitive plants that can easily dominate an ecosystem. A more informal term for invasive plants is weeds. Other terms used interchangeably with invasive plants are exotic species, invaders, or alien plants.

Invasive plant species displace native vegetation, disrupt the ecosystem, and are the equivalent of "biological pavement." They render the habitat as useless to native wildlife as if it were filled with concrete. The effects of invasive plant species are economic losses in the agricultural and nonagricultural sector, loss of wildlife habitat, and loss of endangered plant species.

Invasive plants are so destructive that most states have laws prohibiting their growth or distribution. When a plant is restricted by law, it is referred to as noxious, or harmful, not to be confused with the definition that means "smelly." In some states, a landowner may receive a letter from the local government telling them that they have a noxious weed and they are required to remove it. In some cases, if the landowner will not remove it by mowing or spraying, the government can enter on to the property and do it. The landowner would then be assessed a tax or billed.

LIFE CYCLES OF PLANTS

Plants have one of three life cycles: annual, biennial, or perennial. **Annuals** complete their life in one growing season, **biennials** in two growing seasons, and **perennials** in two or more years. Understanding a plant's life cycle can predict characteristics about a plant's seed production and root growth.

Many times, a plant's life cycle can be determined simply by examining the roots. An annual weed has a shallow root system since it starts out new each season. Biennials have a more substantial root system, many times a **taproot** (Figure 1.1). The taproot is the main part of the root below the ground that gives the plant support. The taproot is usually thick compared with other parts of the root and provides food storage for the plant. Perennials have the most substantial root systems. Have you ever tried to dig out a dandelion and realized that part of the root snapped off? Dandelions are perennials and have deeper root systems than most annuals and biennials. Gardeners are well aware of the deep root system of mature dandelions. Many perennials, such as bindweed (*Convolvulus arvensis*), have modified stems that extend laterally underground. These **rhizomes** are often called "creeping roots" and form an extensive underground network, usually many feet deep.

Annuals

Annuals can be categorized as summer or winter annuals. Most annuals are summer annuals, meaning that they germinate in

Figure 1.1   The taproot gives the plant support by anchoring it into the ground. The taproot is the thick part of the plant just below the surface of the soil.

the spring and flower in the summer. Winter annuals, on the other hand, germinate in the fall, **overwinter**, and grow in the early spring. Overwintering means that the plant survives the winter by going dormant. A dormant plant is still alive, just not actively growing. A dormant plant is similar to a hibernating bear where biological processes are slowed to conserve energy and the living organism relies on stored energy.

Winter annuals have an advantage because they germinate so early (fall versus spring) and tend to get ahead in terms of growth for the season. This "head start" gives plants a competitive edge so it is no surprise that many invasive annuals are winter annuals.

Another noteworthy aspect of annuals is that they reproduce exclusively by seeds. Seeds from annuals, as well as other types of plants, last for many years. When a seed is still able to germinate and become a new plant, it is said to be viable. A seed that remains viable for years is said to have a long seed dormancy.

Ecologists know then that the secret to controlling annuals is to prevent seed production. It is, in fact, more important to prevent seed production for annuals than for other types of plants, because these plants tend to produce vastly greater amounts of seeds. In many cases, seeds are still able to germinate even after seven years. Ninety-one percent of jimsonweed (*Datura stramonium*) seeds were still able to germinate after 38 years. There's an old saying that's still true: One year's seeding equals seven years weeding.

Biennials

Biennials reproduce by seeds and roots. Biennials have a more extensive root system than annuals and they generally resprout unless the full root is pulled out. Biennials are usually a bit more difficult to control because it is hard to remove the entire root system. Many biennials, however, will not flower until the

Figure 1.2   Canada thistle is a perennial with an extensive root system. This invasive plant often appears in clusters initially because of the lateral growth of the roots. One cluster of Canada thistle may appear to be many different plants but, in fact, is just one plant that has sprouted from the lateral roots.

second year of their life, whereas annuals germinate, flower, and set seed all in the same year.

Perennials

Perennials can be long- or short-lived and reproduce by seeds and roots but tend to put more energy into forming a robust root system than high seed production (Figure 1.2). After a deep-soaking rain, many gardeners will often pull and dig the dandelions and other weeds hoping for a better chance of getting the entire root system. Although moist soil will make pulling the root system easier, even a tiny portion of the root system left behind can resprout, especially in moist soil where the plant will take advantage of the available water.

Other perennials, such as bindweed, have root systems so fine that complete root extraction is impossible. The roots of bindweed can extend more than 15 feet below the surface. Digging this deep for bindweed roots will likely do more harm than good since soil disturbance encourages weed seeds and root fragments to germinate. In natural areas, most of the most destructive invasive species tend to be perennials. Control and removal of these invasive plants is difficult due to the extensive root system. Herbicides tend to be most successful on invasive perennials because the chemical moves into the root system and kills the roots.

TERRESTRIAL PLANT SURVIVAL STRATEGIES

All living organisms must aim for survival at the very least. For terrestrial plants, water, nutrients, and sun are the limiting factors that they must compete for.

Fighting for Water

Terrestrial plants need water to maintain their systems and to grow and reproduce. Terrestrial plants absorb water through their roots and excrete or transpire water through the leaves. Desert plants have clever mechanisms to reduce the amount of water that is lost through the leaves since water is precious in these hot and dry climates. One of these mechanisms is a thick **cuticle**. A cuticle is a waterproof layer of cells on the leaves that helps prevent water loss. A cactus has a thick cuticle.

Invasive plants tend to be exceptional at acquiring water. Many deep-rooted invasive plants are able to grow their roots much deeper than native plants. Plants get water from precipitation but mostly get water from underground sources. The water that flows below the soil surface is called **groundwater**. If plants rely primarily on groundwater, deep roots are advantageous to more shallowly rooted ones. Plants that access the belowground water first are better competitors and will be the last ones to die during a drought.

Searching for Nutrients

Plants need large amounts of macronutrients: nitrogen (N), phosphorus (P), and potassium (K). They need smaller amounts of secondary nutrients: calcium (Ca), magnesium (Mg), and sulfur (S). In even smaller quantities they need micronutrients: iron (Fe), manganese (Mn), zinc (Zn), boron (B), copper (Cu), and molybdenum (Mo). Terrestrial plants get these nutrients through their roots. Healthy plants rely on the soil having these nutrients.

Depending on the species of plant, mineral requirements differ. Gardeners know the difficulties of growing azaleas and rhododendrons if the soil is not acidic enough. When a plant has specific requirements for nutrients, it is said to have a narrow niche and when a plant does not have requirements that are scarce, it is said to have a wide niche. A **niche** is defined as the way a species makes its living, or an ecological role in its community.

Invasive plants tend to have wide niches. They are usually adapted to take advantage of the macronutrient nitrogen in the soil and this is why invasive plants are characterized by rapid growth. Sometimes this limits the availability of nitrogen for native plants.

Reaching for the Sun

Without the sun, plants could not make food; they also need a green pigment called chlorophyll along with water and carbon dioxide. With these elements, plants complete the complex process of photosynthesis to make their own food. Photosynthesis can be defined as the process of converting light energy to chemical energy and storing it in the bonds of sugar. Only plants and some algae can photosynthesize.

Photosynthesis occurs in the leaves for most plants, although there are some exceptions. For photosynthesis to occur, there must be chlorophyll, which is a green pigment. Plants vary in their need for sunlight. Some plants tolerate shade; others wither under too much sunlight. Many invasive plants use their ability to grow tall quickly to shade out and compete with other plants. If the plant that cannot grow as quickly as the invasive plant has similar sun requirements, the invasive plant will have the advantage. The result would be that the noninvasive may not thrive without the sunlight it needs.

HOW PLANTS TRAVEL

Nature has ingeniously designed plants to spread their genes as far and wide as possible—and some are better at this than others.[1] Plants travel primarily by seeds. All plants that flower produce seeds—even grasses. Seeds can spread in many ways (Figure 1.3). One way is to attach to the clothes and shoes. Many seeds have miniscule hooks that attach to shoelaces and apparel. Hikers can inadvertently transport the seeds of invasive plants from their campground to the top of a mountain.

A Plant's Home: The World's Biomes

Terrestrial plants can be found in a variety of biomes: grassland, forest, desert, and tundra. Biomes are described as the world's major communities, classified according to predominant vegetation. Each biome requires plants and other organisms to be adapted to the challenging aspects of each of these environments.

Biomes have changed and moved over the course of history due to major changes in climate. Plants are not able to pick up and move like a disgruntled tenant, so they are forced to adapt if they are going to survive. Each biome requires a special set of plant adaptations.

Many people think of deserts as hot places but actually cold deserts occur in the basin and range area of Utah and Nevada. Deserts can be subdivided into four categories: hot and dry, semi-arid, coastal, and cold.

The challenge of life in the desert biome is low annual rainfall. Plants that live in the desert must adapt water-conserving characteristics. Since water is often lost through leaves, most plants develop adaptations to conserve water loss from the leaves. A small leaf with a thick cuticle or outer layer helps to reduce water loss.

The tundra biome is the coldest of all the biomes and is subdivided into arctic and alpine tundra. Arctic tundra is located in the northern hemisphere, including the north pole. Alpine tundra refers to mountaintops throughout the world at high altitudes where trees cannot grow.

The cold climate limits the length of the growing season for plants. In addition, the tundra generally has low species diversity, simple vegetation structure, energy and nutrients in the form of dead organic material, and large fluctuations in the size of populations. Plants adapt to the sweeping winds of the tundra by being short and grouping together to resist the cold temperatures. The snow acts as a protective cover for the plants during the winter. Plants carry out photosynthesis at low temperatures and low light intensities. Because low light intensities restrict growth, plants generally reproduce by budding and division rather than flowering.

Grasslands are lands dominated by grasses rather than shrubs or trees and include tropical grasslands or savannas and temperate grasslands. Soils of the savanna are porous, causing water to drain rapidly. Soils with a higher percentage of sand, versus clay, tend to be porous. The disadvantage of porous soils is that there is usually less organic material because water washes it away. Organic matter provides nutrients for plants. Grasses are better adapted to handle thin soils than trees or shrubs that have a higher nutrient requirement.

Forest biomes are biological communities dominated by trees and can be tropical, temperate, or boreal. Tropical forests are located near the equator and are characterized by the greatest species diversity. Temperate forests have well-defined seasons, particularly winter. Boreal forests or taiga are the largest terrestrial biome, found in the broad belt of Eurasia (the continent that includes Europe and Asia) and North America. Evergreens are the primary vegetation type in the taiga and have adapted to these low temperatures and nutrient-poor soils. Just as their name implies, evergreens never drop their leaves when temperatures cool; they don't have to regrow them in the spring. Keeping their leaves saves a lot of energy since growing new leaves requires a lot of energy. Plants get their energy from nutrients in the soil and sun, neither of which is plentiful in the taiga.

Animals also transport seeds. In the same way they do to clothing, seeds attach to the fur of animals. Animals also transport seeds by consuming the seeds and depositing them elsewhere. Grazing animals such as cattle consume large amounts of seeds by eating grass in pastures. If the pasture contains invasive plants, the seeds of these unwanted plants can be transported as far as the animal is able to travel.

Birds are able to deposit seeds much farther from the invasive plants' origins. Birds eat seeds from plants as a food source and deposit these seeds in flight or on the ground. Oftentimes, new populations of invasive plants will show up under trees or by fencelines where birds like to congregate.

Squirrels are also responsible for helping plants to travel. Squirrels bury nuts that can become a tree. The black walnut tree (*Juglans nigra*) owes much of its distribution to squirrels.

Figure 1.3 Wind is a mechanism for spreading plant seeds. In this picture, the seeds are protected in a capsule until they are mature enough to create a new plant.

Figure 1.4 Many species of plants are described as a tumbleweed due to their ability to easily snap at the base and tumble over land. Tumbling is a plant adaptation to spread seeds over a wider geographical range than if the plant stayed rooted to the ground.

Flotation is another way that seeds can disperse their genes. Cotton is a plant adaptation that enables the plant to travel by water and air. Think of a cotton ball and how it floats on water. The "cotton" parts of the plant are slender, hollow, single-celled hairs that are attached to the seeds as a mechanism for wind and water dispersal. The lightweight hairs help the seed disperse by making it airborne or able to float. In fact, geneticists have established that the presence of wild and cultivated cotton in pre-Columbian America is due to a very early flotation of seed across the oceans, rather than human contact.[2] This is one way that people have profited by plants' mechanisms to travel.

Tumbleweeds are an adaptation for plants to travel (Figure 1.4). Approximately a dozen or so species are designed to break off at the base and disperse seeds while tumbling, usually in the arid West where winds can be swift across grasslands that lack trees to stop their tumbling.

Remember that perennials and some biennials have an additional method for reproducing: root segments. For some plants, cutting up the root into pieces as small as .5 inch (1.3 centimeters) can create a whole new plant. Therefore, a piece of root that is transported to another location can create a new plant population. This can occur through farm or garden equipment that breaks up the soil and can break up root segments. Root segments can be dragged to another field and create a new plant population. The propellers of boats are also an effective mechanism for cutting up root segments of aquatic vegetation and transporting them to areas that create a new invasive plant population.

The most influential agent in the spread of invasive plants has been people. In the early days, many invasive plants were introduced intentionally before the problem of invasive plants was known. Today, the spread is largely accidental and is due to travel.

By nature's design, geographic boundaries such as oceans prevented plants and seeds from finding their way far from their origin. But now, people can easily get on a plane, with an aberrant seed stuck in their sock from hiking, and take it thousands of miles away. The U.S. government attempts to control the migration of seeds and plants across the country and internationally but many seeds are too small to readily detect and can attach to nearly anything, even tires. As long as people continue to travel, invasive plants will continue to land in new ecosystems and potentially challenge the native plants living there.

Plant Competition

2

It is in a plant's nature to thrive and reproduce. Terrestrial plants must acquire food and water as well as ward off predators such as animals and insects while staying rooted in the ground. Plants make their own food through the process of photosynthesis—and for that to happen, plants must be in a location to receive adequate sunlight. These are a few of the challenges plants face.

SECONDARY COMPOUNDS

Plants do not flourish in isolation, but in intimate relationships with many species, from those that feed off them or attack them to those that help their pollination or seed dispersal.[3] Predators are species that attack or feed off plants and are another obstacle to plant growth and reproduction. Fighting predators involves a variety of mechanisms. One way a plant can discourage a hungry animal is by producing toxic or poisonous plant parts. Specialized substances that a plant produces are referred to as secondary compounds. The three major types of secondary compounds are saponins, glycosides, and alkaloids. These chemicals are called secondary because they are produced beyond the requirements of daily growth for seeding, flowering, and maintaining daily function.

Humans are quite fortunate that plants produce secondary compounds to fight predators. Have you ever used an antibiotic?

Plants, Plantations, and Our Commodities

Running late for school once again, you grab an elastic to pull your hair back in a ponytail and just barely catch the bus. Once at school, you grab an eraser to redo a math problem. And to what plant do you owe all these conveniences of tires, fan belt, to run automobiles, and hair ties? Rubber, made from latex, is a secondary alkaloid compound of the rubber plant.

Rubber is gathered by "tapping" the tree, which involves cutting spiral-shaped grooves to the depth of about .25 inch (.6 centimeter) into the bark halfway around the tree. Just halfway though, because cutting the bark all the way around the tree will kill the tree; this is known as girdling. The latex flows down the groove, through a spout, and is collected in a cup. Most of the rubber comes from plantations in Southeast Asia. Women are responsible for much of the rubber tapping. In Sri Lanka, almost half the labor employed in rubber tapping is recruited from nearby villages, and very many of these workers are women.

Rubber tapping is physically exhausting and a typical day's work starts at 6:15 A.M. Many of the women will have risen at around 4 A.M. to fulfill domestic tasks, prepare breakfast, and ensure their

We owe substances such as antibiotics and antihistamines to the fact that plants are extraordinary chemical factories. Certain plant families are known for making specific secondary compounds. Most people are familiar with the stimulating effects of caffeine, yet few people realize it is a secondary compound. Caffeine as well as morphine, quinine, and strychnine are alkaloids, which can be lethal if taken in high doses.

Nicotine is another alkaloid that most people are familiar with. Nicotine is a secondary compound produced by the children are ready for school.* They then set out for a 2- to 3-mile (3.2- to 4.8-kilometer) walk to the plantation, followed by a further trek to reach the designated areas of the plantation for their work. Each woman is required to tap approximately 250 trees a day, the work to be completed by noon, before making a second round of all the trees to harvest the latex that has collected in coconut shells attached to them. The latex is poured into an aluminum bucket, which the woman must then transport over rough terrain—another physically arduous task. Failure to tap the required number of trees results in a woman's meager wages for the day being halved by her employer.

After walking back home, a woman might typically spend the late afternoon collecting firewood in preparation for cooking the evening meal. Some female rubber workers are the sole support of their households, while others may receive scant support from their husbands.

*Toby and Will Musgrave. *Women Workers on Rubber Plantations*. London: Cassell and Company, 2000, p. 175.

tobacco plant (*Nicotiana tabacum*). Although tobacco smoke contains some 4,000 chemicals, botanists were able to isolate and identify nicotine in 1828. Nicotine is tobacco's strongest psychoactive ingredient. It is a high-powered stimulant and one of the most addictive drugs available, comparable to heroin and cocaine, according to the U.S. Surgeon General.[4] Remember that alkaloids are generally toxic or poisonous and nicotine is certainly no exception. For all of its uses and effects on animals, including people, nicotine is made by the tobacco plant to deter insects. Insects are predators because they eat plants and often lay eggs inside the seedhead or other plant parts. Nicotine is so successful as an insecticide that it was regularly used by gardeners in Victorian England. Even today, organic gardeners will soak a cigarette in water overnight, drain and then use the liquid to spray on garden plants as a natural insecticide. Next time someone around you lights up, you may want to let them know they are inhaling an insecticide.

Glycosides are another type of secondary compound. Glycosides consist of a physiologically active molecule linked to a sugar molecule. A physiologically active molecule causes a response such as a contraction in the heart. Cardiac glycosides

Aspirin and Acne: What Willows Have Done for You

The strange story of aspirin is typical of plant research and discovery. Since early times, it was known that the bark of the white willow (*Salix alba*) could kill pain. Decoctions or infusions of it were used against fevers, rheumatic pains, gout, toothache, earache, and headache. The active ingredient was first isolated from willows in the nineteenth century and named salicin. A similar compound, salicylic acid, was isolated from other species of willows with the Latin name of *Spiraea ulmaria*. In 1899, it was found that the combination of salicylic acid and acetic acid—the chemical acetylsalicylic acid—was more effective. This new substance was then confusingly named "aspirin" after *Spiraea*. Salicylic acid is still used today for acne and athlete's foot.*

*Anthony Huxley. *Green Inheritance. The World Wildlife Fund Book of Plants.* New York: Doubleday, 1985, pp. 11–23, 91, 115.

are used in heart treatment. Although cardiac glycosides have beneficial uses for the heart, they can also have toxic effects. Plants that produce glycosides have been used as both poison and heart drugs. There is an old saying that is true when considering the effects of these compounds: The poison is in the dose. A cup of coffee won't kill you, nor will a dash of salt, but much larger doses of each can be fatal. Plants produce these compounds in amounts designed to be toxic or poisonous to their predators.

Saponins have a distinctive foaming characteristic. Soapwort (*Saponaria*) contains saponin and the roots were historically used as a soap. The Latin name for the plant, *Saponaria* comes from the Latin for soap: *sapo*. Plants put energy into making saponins because these chemicals taste bitter to livestock. Livestock will avoid plants that contain saponins because they quickly learn that these plants do not taste good. Saponins are more than just unpleasant tasting; plants that contain high levels of saponins can cause life-threatening toxicity for livestock. And what plants would you guess tend to accumulate saponins? Plants that are likely to be grazed, of course. Alfalfa, which is generally grown for its high forage value, contains several saponins. Saponin content in alfalfa tends to be low in the spring and fall and highest in mid-summer.

St. John's wort is a toxic perennial plant found in natural areas that causes photosensitivity in cattle when eaten. Photosensitivity is caused by alkaloids in the plant that heighten the skin's sensitivity to light, resulting in severe sunburns particularly in light-skinned animals. Just as very light-skinned people are usually more sensitive to the sun, so are animals. Ranchers have noted that the light-skinned areas of cows will peel off in sheets after eating St. John's wort (*Hypericum perforatum*), whereas the darker areas will be fine. The areas of the animal that are affected by photosensitivity can become painfully infected.

Myrtle spurge (*Euphorbia myrsinites*) causes permanent scarring of the skin when the milky latex (alkaloid) touches the skin (Figure 2.1). This plant was introduced as an ornamental but is difficult to contain and has begun to invade native ecosystems.

Water hemlock (*Cicuta douglasii*) is a poisonous plant found in wet meadows, riverbanks, and alleyways in the West. The difference between toxic and poisonous is that toxicity causes irritation or illness and poisonous plant parts will lead to death if consumed. Water hemlock is one of the most poisonous plants in North America. A compound called cicutoxin is the cause of muscle tremors and violent convulsions that animals (including

Figure 2.1 Myrtle spurge is an invasive plant that contains a toxic liquid in the stems and leaves. When broken, the milky liquid oozes out of the plant and can cause permanent scarring to the skin. Animals will not eat myrtle spurge and therefore this plant has become extremely difficult to control.

people) will experience. Once the animal consumes the plant, there is no antidote and death will occur within three hours.

Whether toxic or poisonous, predators learn to avoid these plants. Remember the saying for poison ivy: Leaves of three, let them be. The advantage of deterring predators is that the plant has a better chance of not only being able to grow, but to flower and produce seeds.

ADAPTATIONS

A plant's drive to grow and reproduce can be displayed by its ability to adapt. **Adaptations** are small changes a plant makes over time to better compete in its environment. It is clear that just any set of features on a plant will not do. The species would not thrive, would probably not reproduce, and would then go extinct. It is clear then that the set of features we see on a plant are ones that have been successful in the course of evolution.

Thorns on roses are one type of adaptation. Thorns are actually modified leaves. The thorns help protect the plant. Another example of a modification is the shape of rain forest leaves. The drip tips of rain forest leaves have adapted to cope with high levels of rainfall. The tip is shaped in a way that allows raindrops to run off quickly. This adaptation helps prevent fungus and bacteria from growing on the leaves, which is a particular concern in a warm and wet environment. These modifications are another way that a plant can be competitive in its environment and ensure completion of its life cycle.

HOW THEY COMPETE

Plants share resources in an environment where resources are limited. All plants need water and there is only so much rainfall and groundwater. This situation leads to competition. Two main distinctions are made in describing how plants compete. One method is referred to as **exploitative**, where plants obtain resources more efficiently and rapidly than other species. Another way is **interference**, where plants use antagonistic or fighting behavior such as noxious chemicals to exclude species from an area.

Plants use distinct mechanisms to gain an edge. Certain attributes tend to make a plant more competitive than others. Of course, it depends on the environment. Labrador tea (*Ledum groenlandicum*) evolved on tundras early on when the Earth was covered in ice. Although the planet has warmed, this plant still grows on craggy summits in northern latitudes.

Who Controls the Movement of Plants Through Borders?

The U.S. Department of Agriculture's (USDA) Animal and Plant Health Inspection Service (APHIS) is responsible for ensuring that plants that enter this country are free from pests and diseases. APHIS inspects plants that are mailed, carried, or shipped into this country by travelers and nursery owners.

APHIS asks every international traveler as they go through customs if they are carrying plant parts in their suitcase. It takes the actions of only one person to introduce an invasive species that could have devastating impacts on an ecosystem.

Another place that APHIS inspects for foreign plants is ports of entry. At these plant inspection stations, inspectors work with specialists in the fields of entomology, botany, and plant pathology to locate, examine, and identify exotic pests, diseases, and noxious weeds. Entomology is the study of insects; botany is the study of plants; and plant pathology is the study of plant disease.

APHIS is not trying to completely eliminate the introduction of foreign plants. After all, many of the plants people buy in nurseries

Labrador tea would be competitive at the top of the highest Vermont mountain but would do poorly in the bayou of Louisiana. Even so, some generalizations can be made about plant competition.

Not all competition is the same. **Intraspecific competition** occurs between plants of the same species. Two Canada thistle (*Cirsium arvense*) plants growing side by side are competing for resources such as sun, water, and nutrients. **Interspecific competition** occurs between members of different species. Black walnut (*Juglans nigra*) is a valuable lumber tree that is also

for their gardens have been imported from other countries. Many fruits and vegetables also have been imported. APHIS ensures the safety of these imports with a few precautionary steps.

The first requirement that a person must fulfill is to apply for an agricultural import permit and secure a phytosanitary certificate from the exporting country. Phytosanitary certificates verify that plant quarantine officials from the exporting country have examined the plants for pests and diseases prior to exporting them. Once the plant arrives in the U.S. port, an inspector examines samples from each species of plant and seed. The inspection process includes a meticulous examination of the leaves, stems, roots, and seeds of the plant.

If an inspector does discover a pest, disease, or noxious weed, he or she determines the extent of the harm they could cause. Plant pests that are identified as not existing in the United States or existing in a limited extent, are quarantined, exported, or destroyed.

grown as a shade tree and for its highly nutritious and edible nuts. Black walnut produces a chemical called "juglone," which occurs naturally in all parts of the tree. Juglone is released into the soil and this chemical inhibits respiration in other plants. Inhibiting respiration deprives other plants of needed energy for metabolic activity. Plants that grow near black walnut and are sensitive to juglone will begin to yellow, wilt, and eventually die. This process where one plant produces a chemical that inhibits the growth of another plant is called **allelopathy**. Allelopathy is interference because the plant is using chemicals to exclude species from their area.

THE QUALITIES OF AN OUTSTANDING COMPETITOR

One competitive quality is how quickly a plant can grow. Some plants take a year to grow an inch (2.54 centimeters); others can grow a foot (.3 meter) in a couple of months. Have you ever planted a spruce or pine tree? Those trees tend to grow more slowly but tend to live longer than more rapidly growing perennials such as aspens or willows.

Plants that can take advantage of rapid growth tend to be more prolific. Plants that can establish and grow quickly will shade out slower-growing plants. In addition, if the more rapidly growing plants have established roots and there is a drought, the shallower-rooted plant will suffer from lack of water.

Rapid growth tends to be pivotal after disturbance. Examples of disturbance are flood, fire, plowing, or anything that causes an upheaval to the land. Plants that arrive early after a disturbance by seed or root segment will have an advantage in dominating the new landscape, but being able to grow rapidly is also critical.

Producing a lot of seeds is another quality that makes a plant competitive. All flowering plants produce seeds. As mentioned, seeds are an important way for plants to begin new populations in distant locations. Different species of plants produce different numbers of seeds. Some produce a bounty of seeds while others are more sparing. Each flower produces seeds and many plants have more than one flower on a single plant. Musk thistle (*Carduus nutans*) produces nearly a million seeds per plant. Seeds have requirements for growth, just like a mature plant does. Seeds need the right temperature, moisture level, and usually light. However, 15% of plant species have seeds that can germinate in darkness, and Russian thistle (*Salsola iberica*) seeds have been known to germinate on ice. Assuming there is no shortage of moisture, plants with the most seeds will have the greatest chance of dominating a landscape, at least in the beginning. These plants will need other survival strategies to make sure their seedlings grow and reproduce in the environment where they germinated.

THE INVASIVE SPECIES ADVANTAGE: AWAY FROM HOME WITHOUT THEIR ENEMIES

As discussed, invasive species tend to be more competitive in the ecosystem. Their competitive edge is attributable to the lack of natural predators such as insects and disease pathogens. They have the additional advantage of freed-up energy that otherwise would be spent on fighting disease or insects. Invasive plants can put this additional energy into evolving into a more fit species overall.

Plants are constantly changing, evolving into a better species to adapt to changes in their environment. Invasives tend to acquire adaptations more quickly. Scientists have taken samples of invasive plant species in the United States and then traveled back to their native countries to take samples. The two populations are found to be genetically different using DNA testing, just like two people that are related may be similar but their DNA is different. The plant population that is in its nonnative environment appears more fit, meaning that it is able to grow more rapidly, reproduce, and acquire nutrients more efficiently. It makes sense that two populations of plants separated by many thousands of miles and growing in different ecosystems would be genetically different since plants are constantly evolving in response to their environment.

By Sea and by Land

3

• •

Invasive terrestrial plants came to the United States as seeds and plant parts buried in hay bales, in the suitcases of immigrants, and on other animals and products shipped overseas. Some plants were introduced because they were thought to be of value in their new home; those are the intentional introductions. Other invasive plants were inadvertently introduced because their seeds or plant parts were attached to animals, people, or things that made their way to the ecosystems of the United States.

ACCIDENTAL INTRODUCTIONS

Today, we are aware of the problem of introducing nonnative or alien species, yet it still continues. Accidental introductions of exotic species pose a huge threat to the economy and also to native plants and animals. A major source of accidental introductions is sea ballast water from cargo ships.

Hitchhikers in Hay

Horses and cattle around the country eat hay as a supplement to grass in their pastures. Oftentimes, these animals are confined to pastures too small for there to be enough grass to meet their nutritional needs. A plant such as alfalfa (*Medicago sativa*) is grown in fields elsewhere and when it has grown enough, the alfalfa is cut, left to dry, and then baled as hay to be purchased.

Like many crops, alfalfa fields contain weeds or invasive species. When alfalfa is cut and baled, the weeds and their seeds get scooped up along with the rest of the vegetation. Bales are often taken many miles away with the weed seeds contained within the bale. Seeds either fall to the ground to germinate or are eaten by the animal and passed through. Seeds that pass through the bodies of animals are often still able to produce a plant. Most seeds are still able to germinate and become a new plant even though they may lay dormant for years. The problem of weed seed dispersal in hay has been a problem since the 1800s and continues today.

What Actions Are Being Taken Today to Prevent Invasive Species Introductions?

Prevention is the focus of invasive species management. In addition to cautionary measures such as using certified weed-free seed, mulch, and hay and monitoring plants that are imported, the National Aeronautics Space Administration (NASA) is helping the federal land management agencies to predict where invasive species may be. By providing observations of the Earth and building predictive models resulting from satellite research, NASA can enhance land managers' capabilities to respond to the challenge of controlling invasive species. NASA has already had success in predicting invasive plants in Utah's Grand Staircase-Escalante Monument. The U.S. Geological Survey (USGS) was using predictive maps to determine where invasive species may spread next. NASA was able to enhance these maps by collecting data from their Terra satellite that provides daily information about vegetative conditions. The satellite detects sunlight reflected by different plants and the environments in which they are growing. Each

One of the best defenses against weed dispersal from hay is to purchase certified weed-free hay. Hay that is certified weed-free is inspected before it is harvested to verify that there are no propagative plant parts.

INTENTIONAL INTRODUCTIONS

Many of today's invasive species were introduced to this country simply because they were desirable in some way. Some were introduced because they were pretty, others because they helped stabilize the soil. Plants that grow tall quickly were used to break

plant has a different appearance in the image created by the satellite which allows scientists to determine an invasive plant's current location and areas that may develop a future invasion.

The improved mapping system will be used to forecast new infestations and to develop a rapid response to eradicate the invaders. This forecasting and rapid response program is called the National Invasive Species Forecasting System (NISFS). The NISFS is an online tool for users to combine information about the local presence of an invasive species with observations and the predictions from NASA and other sources. The NISFS can generate a regional view of the distribution of an invasive species and predict where it is likely to spread. The NISFS will provide on-demand, local assessments of invasive species patterns and vulnerable habitats, information that is vital for detection, remediation, and management of invasive species.

Figure 3.1 Many invasive plants, such as yellow toadflax, have a beautiful flower. These ornamental plants were introduced from other countries where they escaped gardens and have spread. Yellow toadflax displaces native plants and provides little value as food for foraging animals.

up wind that could also lead to soil erosion. At the time, nobody realized the problems that these species would cause.

Escaped Ornamentals

Ornamental plants beautify our gardens, roadsides, and parks. Summer blossoms are generally showy flowers that attract people as well as pollinating insects. Ornamentals are planted and cultivated by people to encourage their growth. Many invasive plants have eye-catching, showy flowers. Before the problem with invasive plants was known, many invasives were introduced simply because they were beautiful. These exotic ornamentals escape the confines of their terrain and do damage to the ecosystems they invade. Although these plants may look delicate, they become aggressive and outcompete their native neighbors.

Figure 3.2 Kudzu is an invasive plant that was introduced by the federal government to reduce soil erosion in the South. Kudzu is an aggressive, invasive vine and will grow over almost any stationary object.

> ### Kudzu: The Plant That Ate the South
>
> Kudzu (*Pueraria montana* var. *lobata*) is an all-too-familiar weed in the Southeast. Kudzu, originally from Asia, is a climbing perennial vine that can be found covering almost anything that has remained stationary for any length of time. Stop signs and abandoned cars are sometimes barely recognizable under a thick blanket of leaf-lets, purple flowers, and eventually hairy, flattened seedpods.
>
> One way that kudzu is competitive is through rapid growth. Once established, kudzu may extend as much as 60 feet (18 meters) per season at a rate of one foot per day! Each kudzu vine can be up to 100 feet (30 meters) long and .5 to 4 inches (1 to 10 centimeters) thick. The roots of this perennial are fleshy and have massive taproots that are 7 inches (18 centimeters) or more in diameter and weigh as much as 400 pounds (181 kilograms). As a perennial, kudzu can reproduce by modified stems called runners. Runners appear aboveground. Strawberry plants are an example of a plant with runners. Kudzu also has modi-fied stems called rhizomes. These rhizomes are often called "creeping

Butter-and-Eggs: Anything but Edible

Yellow toadflax (*Linaria vulgaris*) is referred to as butter-and-eggs because the beautiful flowers resemble the light and dark hues of butter and eggs (Figure 3.1). Yellow toadflax, originally from Eurasia (the continent that includes Europe and Asia), has proliferated since the early 1800s. This invasive plant was highly valuable in its native country, where it was used for fabric dyes and for medicinal purposes. Unfortunately, this invasive continues to displace native vegetation.

It grows well in rangelands and pastures of the West but has also spread to mountains and parks. Of particular concern is that this weed is not eaten by native wildlife or even cattle.

roots," although they are not actually roots. Segmented portions of the rhizomes that contain a node can become a new kudzu plant. The hairy, flattened seedpods also contain three to ten hard seeds where one or two are able to germinate and become a new plant.

Another way that kudzu maintains its abundant growth is by growing in areas where sunlight is plentiful and winters are mild. Kudzu's preferred habitats are abandoned fields, roadsides, and forest edges, all locations in direct sun.

Kudzu was intentionally introduced in the late 1800s to provide forage for grazing animals and as an ornamental plant. During the mid-1900s, Franklin D. Roosevelt's Civilian Conservation Corps planted it extensively because it was believed to help prevent soil erosion. Its rapid growth and extensive root system did help stabilize soil but the U.S. government quickly learned the folly of their introduction and kudzu was soon thereafter listed as a pest. It is now illegal to plant it.

The leaves of yellow toadflax have a thick, waxy cuticle that accounts for the unpalatable nature of this plant. Rangelands and pastures are lands where grazing animals find food. As more grasses are displaced by yellow toadflax, there will be less food for these animals.

Soil Stabilizers

Many invasive terrestrial plants were introduced because they were thought to provide a benefit to barren areas. People were impressed by how quickly they established themselves. Lands without any vegetation tend to have soil loss or erosion. Recognizing that soil is an important natural resource, invasive plants such as kudzu (*Pueraria montana* var. *lobata*) were brought in to stabilize the soil in areas without vegetation (Figure 3.2).

Windbreaks or Shelterbelts

The third category is plants that were intentionally introduced as windbreaks or shelterbelts. Windbreaks consist of a linear arrangement of trees and shrubs. Shelterbelts are multiple rows (four or more) of trees and shrubs. Plants in windbreaks or shelterbelts do exactly what the name implies; they break up strong gusts of wind. The importance of halting the velocity of the wind is that, similar to soil stabilizers, it helps to reduce soil erosion. Stronger gusts are more able to move soil particles. Heavy windstorms can lead to a severe loss of precious soils, particularly on farms. Lining a farm with sturdy, tall trees that establish quickly provides the best windbreak. Siberian elm (*Ulmus pumila*) was introduced for this purpose and continues to thrive in the arid West, displacing native trees that are much slower growing.

Biological Control

INTRODUCING THE ENEMY

4

● ●

The main problem with invasive species is that they lack their natural predators because they arrived here without them. So the simple solution should be to find those natural predators and bring them here, right? As with any so-called simple solution to a complex environmental problem, it is not that easy.

Introducing an insect that is a predator to control an invasive plant is described as a biological control technique. Another type of control would be spraying an invasive with herbicides to kill it; this is known as chemical control.

INTRODUCING BIOLOGICAL CONTROL AGENTS: THE BENEFITS AND THE RISKS

The danger of biological control is that it requires introducing another nonnative species to solve the original problem of an exotic introduction. This new species could become a pest as well and potentially more difficult to control.

The classic "oops" biological control story does not involve insects but instead, the mongoose. The small Indian mongoose (*Herpestes auropunctatus*) is a slender animal with short legs and well-developed teeth used to tear flesh. This animal was introduced into Hawaii during the 1870s to control Norway rats in sugarcane. The mongoose ate the Norway rats but did not eat the tree rat because the mongoose couldn't climb trees. The Norway

43

Insectaries: Where the Insects Are Born

It takes more than just a few insects to initiate a new population. Most insect releases require hundreds, if not thousands, of insects to be released all in the same spot. Land managers need to solicit the help of breeders to get the number of insects they need. Insects naturally breed in the field but can also be bred in a lab, called an insectary. Governmental and private agencies maintain insectaries to supply insects for biological control of gardens, farms, stables, pastures, and compost yards.

Insectaries generally distribute the insects they breed many miles away. Insects are packaged in waxless ice cream containers or paper bags and kept in a cooler. Insects are very active and cool conditions will help minimize the chance that they will escape and die in transit. Once the insects arrive at their destination, the bag is emptied; the insects resume eating and ideally lay eggs that will overwinter and become adults next season.

Field insectary site (FIS) colonies have been established by the U.S. Forest Service. As the name implies, these insectaries are outdoors

rat and tree rat were competitors and because the Norway rat was being eliminated, the tree rat was able to increase in number and became a pest in Hawaii. The mongoose also ate snakes and snake eggs, decreasing the snakes that were previously controlling the tree rats. As if all of that wasn't bad enough, the mongoose then became a pest in Puerto Rico where it ate chickens and waterfowl and also became a vector (carrier) for rabies. It is estimated that this mongoose is causing $50 million in damages annually in Puerto Rico and the Hawaiian Islands alone.[5] Much has been learned since the 1870s however, and mistakes like the intentional introduction of the mongoose do not happen anymore.

and the insects are bred in such high numbers that the removal of some to a new location does not hinder weed control efforts. Actually, removing excess insects from a highly populated site helps weed control efforts because it prevents the insect population from "crashing," or rapidly declining in number. Many of these FIS colonies become so successful that their management is turned over to state departments of agriculture, and university, county, and federal land managers with weed control responsibilities. The benefit of FIS colonies over private insectaries is that the insects are free as long as someone is willing to collect them. Private insectaries charge for their insects. Prices range, but they can be up to one dollar per insect.

Using a lab to rear biological control agents has the advantage of manipulating temperature, humidity, and light. Outdoor insectaries cannot be controlled for environmental influences. Scientists can also use labs to learn additionally about the best conditions for releasing insects such as soil type and weed stand density. Labs can reveal important information to make better releases in the field.

The biggest concern is that a plant with economic significance could be affected, such as a crop plant. Luckily, scientists have experiments that can ensure that the insect will eat only the plant it was intended to. These experiments can take up to ten years to complete. Even with that, there are no guarantees; nobody knows for sure how the insect will act in a real-world environment as opposed to in a lab.

Scientists will recommend introducing insects as biological control agents that will eat only the invasive plant (Figure 4.1). They test for this by keeping the insect in a confined area and offering it a variety of plants. The plants that an insect is willing

Figure 4.1 Introducing a plant's natural enemy, such as an insect, is referred to as biological control. Ideally, the introduced insect will eat the invasive plant and nothing else. Scientists do many experiments to be sure that the introduced biological control agent will not become a pest itself.

to eat or parasitize are referred to as its **host range**. Scientists make sure that the insect they are introducing as a biological control has a host range that is restricted to the invasive plant.

Some of the experiments involve withholding any plants that the insect would eat and offering a crop or other valuable plant to see if the insect will eat it if it only has a choice between eating the valuable plant or starvation. Insects are kept in cages to carefully monitor what they are eating. If the insect is willing to starve before eating the other plant, it increases its chances of being considered suitable for introduction.

PREDATOR-PREY RELATIONSHIPS

Predator-prey relationships are the interactions where one species is a food source or prey for the other species. A predator is the animal that eats the other. Prey is the animal that the predator is eating. Predators and prey in action have been depicted on nature shows on TV where the cheetah outruns the gazelle, which gets eaten. Although not quite as dramatic, insects and plants have predator-prey relationships as well (Figure 4.2).

Predators and prey evolve together and occur naturally in the environment. The predator encourages the fittest of the prey species. Prey will try to avoid being eaten and will therefore develop characteristics to prevent death. The prey may evolve to be faster if the predator is a chasing animal. The prey may also develop a better sense of smell, sight, or camouflage. Characteristics that the prey possesses that do not enable them to escape the predator would not be improved or refined. Similarly, characteristics that predators have that enable them to catch their prey, like claws, sharp teeth, and keen eyesight, would be developed over time.

Predator-prey relationships are nature's way of keeping species in balance. The predator's population may be larger than usual one season but will decrease because of the limits on food (the prey). Separating the predator from its prey knocks the system

Figure 4.2 The predator-prey relationship is nature's way of keeping populations in balance. The Venus flytrap is the predator that has caught its prey: the ladybug.

out of balance and causes a potentially damaging situation for the environment. A "superspecies" may come to dominate where there are few controls on the population.

CONTROLLING ST. JOHN'S WORT WITH BEETLES

The introduction of Chrysolina beetles (*Chrysolina ssp.*) to control the invasive plant St. John's wort is a biological control success story. The flea beetles control leafy spurge by feeding on the foliage when the insect is in the adult and larval stages. Before this insect matures, it spends its life as larvae. The injury that the larvae and adult insects does to the plants makes them more susceptible to disease by allowing pathogens to enter the plants. The insects and disease help to control the population of the plant.

The advantage of using beetles for the control of St. John's wort is that it provides a long-term solution, unlike chemical applications. The drawback, however, is that results are not immediate and complete eradication is never attained.

Significant reductions in invasive plants may take three to eight years, assuming that the original insect population survives and continues to reproduce. As stated, biological control will never completely get rid of the invasive plants because the plants and insects are an example of a predator-prey relationship where both populations naturally fluctuate.

Beetles will travel to other St. John's wort infestations, but human intervention can speed up the process. Insect populations may reach numbers large enough to harvest and relocate to other St. John's wort populations. A sweep net is used to collect insects and redistribute them to other areas. Redistributing insects may seem tedious but once populations are well established and feasting on the invasive plant, there is little intervention required, unlike herbicides that have to be applied year after year.

5 Spotted Knapweed
PRODUCING POISONS

• •

In the early 1900s, spotted knapweed (*Centaura maculosa*) was accidentally introduced from Eastern Europe to the United States as a contaminant in crop seed. Since then it has spread to millions of acres, primarily in the West but also in the East.

Spotted knapweed is an invasive biennial or short-lived perennial that invades pastures, rangelands, and fallowlands (Figure 5.1). Pastures and **rangelands** are grazing lands most common in the western United States, but **pastures** generally have some sort of improvement on the land such as fencing. **Fallowlands** are previously farmed croplands. Most farmers alternate years that they farm their ground. One year they may farm with wheat and the next year they would not plant any crops. Letting a field remain fallow prevents depleting the soil of its nutrients but allows for the growth of weeds. Back in the early 1900s, farmers continuously farmed their grounds. The soil became so depleted that it dried up and blew away. This devastating situation was called the Dust Bowl and was fictionalized in John Steinbeck's classic novel, *The Grapes of Wrath*.

Today, most spotted knapweed is spread as a contaminant in hay, or pieces of the plant are driven miles on the undercarriages of vehicles. If the branches contain viable seeds, new spotted knapweed populations can grow wherever seeds drop from the underside of the car.

Figure 5.1 Spotted knapweed is a common invasive plant on rangelands in the western United States. It was accidentally introduced, probably by seed caught in imported hay. Spotted knapweed seeds continue to be transported in hay, causing new populations to sprout up across the West.

WHAT DAMAGE DOES SPOTTED KNAPWEED CAUSE?

Spotted knapweed grows rapidly both aboveground in the form of leaves, shoots, or actively growing twigs or stems, flowers, and seeds, and belowground in the form of roots. Spotted knapweed's growth is described as aggressive because it takes a large quantity of the resources to grow and occupies a lot of space. Valuable forage grasses, crops, and native plants tend to reduce their growth because of a lack of water, space, or nutrients. **Monocultures** (fields of one plant species) of spotted knapweed are particularly common in western states (Figure 5.2). Monocultures are undesirable in nature because there is no diversity of species. Ecosystems are valued for their rich diversity of species or biological diversity. When ecosystems have a multitude of species to rely on, it is less likely that a particular disease or predator can disrupt the function of the entire system. By creating monocultures, invasive terrestrial plants reduce biological diversity. As discussed, spotted knapweed, similar to many other invasives, was introduced without its natural predators and is therefore able to grow vastly out of control.

Spotted knapweed is allelopathic. Allelopathy enables a plant to produce chemicals from its roots that inhibit the growth of other plants. The plant produces a natural herbicide to compete with other plants. Even after the spotted knapweed is removed from the ground, the soil will still contain the chemicals that will inhibit the growth of other plants. This makes restoration of lands that are infested with spotted knapweed even more difficult. The chemicals must break down or biodegrade before other plant species could be successfully introduced to this soil. The time it takes for these chemicals to biodegrade depends on factors that contribute to decomposition, such as precipitation. Climates such as the arid

West (Arizona, Utah) are places where decomposition rates are slower because of low precipitation; that is why Indian ruins are able to survive there for thousands of years.

Another way that allelopathic chemicals can be encouraged to decompose is by tillage. **Tillage** uses plows or discs to cut up and bury plant parts. Tillage turns soil over and exposes the soil to air that helps break down the chemical compounds in the soil. Farmers use tillage to control weeds and to provide the seedbed for planting crops. The disadvantage of tillage is that exposing the soil to the air can dry it out. In areas where water is relied on mostly through irrigation, tillage is reduced to conserve water. The practice of reducing tillage is known as conservation tillage.

Figure 5.2   Many invasive plants dominate rangeland in the western United States, where they are able to grow to the exclusion of native plants. This problem poses a burden to ranchers because most invasive plants are distasteful to foraging animals.

Catechin: The New Organic Herbicide?

An extract from the green tea many people drink may soon be used as a natural herbicide. Scientists have isolated a root extract from spotted knapweed that is as powerful as the chemical weed killer found in most residential herbicides.

Scientists have known for decades that spotted knapweed releases natural herbicides from the roots. This process is known as allelopathy and is a competitive strategy against other plants. Allelopathy in spotted knapweed prevents the growth of competing plants—even its close relative, diffuse knapweed (*Centaurea diffusa*). Spotted knapweed, however, does not suffer when exposed to its own root extracts. Scientists have now isolated the compound responsible for this activity: catechin.

Catechin has antioxidant properties and is found in green tea. Antioxidants are believed to help prevent cancer because of their ability to destroy harmful molecules known as free radicals. Catechin kills the root tips of other plants, which eventually causes the entire plant to die. Just as blood flows through our bodies, plants have cytoplasm that flows within the cell walls. This movement of cytoplasm in plant cells is referred to as "streaming." Catechin immediately stops cytoplasmic streaming. If blood were to stop flowing in our bodies, we would die. Similarly, when cytoplasm stops flowing in a plant, it dies.

Spotted knapweed does not make good food for native wildlife such as elk. Native wildlife evolved with native plant life and both help support to the other's population. Outsiders such as spotted knapweed do not always make a good replacement for these native plants. Native wildlife are left with few options if there are barely any forage grasses in a field

A plant's response to catechin is fairly rapid. It takes approximately 30 seconds for the root cap to sense catechin. The death of cells begins at the root cap and proceeds from the bottom to the top of the plant in 20 minutes. Complete death of plants tested occurred in 14 days. Another advantage of catechin is that grasses are tolerant of its effects. Catechin could be sprayed on a lawn or pasture without fear of injuring desirable species.

Many people are more comfortable with the idea of applying chemicals made by nature rather than the artificially created synthetic chemicals used in herbicides. Catechin's method of killing plants seems more benign than that of synthetic herbicides. Most residential herbicides kill plants by disrupting cell growth—essentially causing a cancerlike growth in the plant. This process has long concerned opponents of synthetic herbicides.

This product is not yet available to the home gardener but should be soon. Coincidentally, a company that makes green tea already manufactures catechin. The catechin is a by-product and is not sold. Catechin would have to pass the EPA's registration process to be sold as an herbicide. Herbicide registration by the EPA is generally a lengthy process but because catechin is a plant derivative, the review period is considerably less than for synthetic herbicides.

of spotted knapweed. Animals would be forced to move on to find food, providing the opportunity for starvation. Acres of spotted knapweed would be left behind as unsuitable habitat for many of these animals.

Spotted knapweed can also cause hives in people. People who have burned it or worked in dense fields of it have complained of

Allergic Reactions to Plants

Spotted knapweed can deliver a very uncomfortable case of hives to an unsuspecting outdoor enthusiast. We all know to avoid poison ivy and oak, but spotted knapweed can be just as uncomfortable.

As with many allergy-inducing plants, sensitivity to spotted knapweed develops through exposure. The first time you come into contact with it, you will have no reaction; by the tenth time you may be itching and reaching for a soothing ointment.

Hives can develop quickly after contact with the plant. A quick rinse with rubbing alcohol should be followed by rinsing with cold water. Do not wipe the infected skin with water first because the chemical compound that causes the hives does not dissolve in water. Remember, rinse, don't wipe; this will prevent the oil from spreading. If needed, oral antihistamines can help. If you are a vegetable gardener, avoid the poisonous leaves of potatoes, tomatoes, and rhubarb; those plants can also cause an irritating rash.

a taste of metal in their mouth. Creating compounds that cause allergic reactions is another way plants repel possible predators, in this case, people.

HOW CAN SPOTTED KNAPWEED BE CONTROLLED?

Small infestations of spotted knapweed can be hand-pulled since the root system is not that extensive in a biennial or short-lived perennial. However, if a piece of the taproot breaks off, the weed can resprout.

Luckily there are biological control agents that can be used to control spotted knapweed. Scientists believe it will take nearly a dozen different species of insects to reduce spotted knapweed populations. Seedhead flies (*Urophora affinis* and *U. quadrifasciata*) have been released with some success. These flies cause spotted knapweed to produce fewer viable seeds and abort flowering.

Plants, Insects, and Chemistry: Infochemicals

A corn earworm caterpillar is eating a cotton leaf plant. The caterpillar drools just a bit, alerting the plant to the presence of volicitin, which is a chemical compound found only in the insect's oral secretions. The volicitin acts as a "signal" to the plant. The cotton plant then releases a blend of volatile compounds. This signature scent is recognized by a parasitic insect indicating the presence of a caterpillar. The parasitic insect responds by depositing her eggs within the caterpillar. The larvae eventually eat the caterpillar. Both the plant and the parasitic insect benefit from this interaction. A relationship where both species benefit is called a mutualistic relationship. In contrast, a relationship where only one species benefits is described as parasitic.

The chemical compounds released by the plant are called terpenes. Smell a rose. Its fragrance is due to the volatility of terpenes. Parasitic insects find their food through terpene cues. Plants defend themselves based on their ability to produce terpenes. A clever strategy, given that the plant must create a defense system while staying rooted in the same location.

(continues)

(continued)

Insects also use volatile compounds to find the best place to lay their eggs. Female parasitic wasps must find a host, such as a caterpillar, to inject their eggs. This process paralyzes the caterpillar while the larvae grow inside and feed on the host.

Compounds such as these are infochemicals. Pheromones are a particular type of infochemical released within species for reproductive purposes. Next time a mosquito lands on your windshield or window, look to see if it is male or female. A male has tiny hairs on his antennae. These hair-like structures catch the molecules of the pheromones of the female.

These infochemicals are responsible for the interactions among plants, herbivore insects, and predatory insects. If left to chance, a wasp could spend her entire life searching for a host for her eggs. Without infochemicals, many predatory insects would not survive.

We also rely on infochemicals. Smell is based on interactions between molecules and receptors in the appropriate organs. Simply stated, smell identifies what is good—apple pie in the oven; and what is bad—sweaty gym socks and rotten food. Smell also identifies us; our odor is as unique to each one of us as a fingerprint.

Another option for controlling spotted knapweed is herbicides. Herbicides are often the cheapest and quickest way to control invasive species infestations; however, their use is controversial. Some scientists feel that herbicides contribute to polluting our environment because the chemicals cause changes in plant cells that mimic cancer. Others feel that, although these herbicides could cause harm to the environment if not properly used, their monitored use and certification by the U.S. Environmental Protection Agency (EPA) can contribute to improving our environment by controlling invasive plants.

6

Saltcedar
DRYING UP RIVERS

• • • • • • • • • • • • • • • • • •

Saltcedar (*Tamarix ramosissima, T. chinensis, T. parviflora*), also called tamarisk, consists of three species of nonnative woody shrubs that were intentionally brought to the United States in the early 1800s. Saltcedar is believed to be from the Mediterranean region eastward across the Middle East to China and Japan. Saltcedar escaped cultivation and spread to the Southwest, predominantly in Arizona and New Mexico.

Upon early introduction, saltcedar was an easy and attractive shrub to establish. Saltcedar resembled a cedar tree with white to pink flowers and grew to 30 feet (9 meters). In fact, saltcedar was planted in some areas simply as an ornamental tree. The dangers of introducing nonnative plants were not known in the early 1800s.

WHY WAS SALTCEDAR IMPORTED?

The U.S. government introduced saltcedar because it was a good soil stabilizer and windbreak (Figure 6.1). **Soil stabilizers** fight erosion because they have extensive root systems that grab on to the soil. A windbreak also helps prevent soil erosion by slowing down the wind's velocity. The higher the wind speed, the more soil that will disperse. At the time, no one knew that saltcedar would become such an aggressive competitor that it would crowd out native trees, shrubs, and broadleaf plants.

WHAT ARE SALTCEDAR'S UNIQUE CHARACTERISTICS?

Like many invasive plants, saltcedar can thrive in a variety of environments. It is particularly competitive along waterways.

Figure 6.1 Saltcedar can quickly dominate riverways, leaving native animals in jeopardy for habitat and seeds as a source of food. Saltcedar is a mighty competitor because of its deep root system and the ability to make the surrounding soil more salty and therefore less hospitable to native plants. Riverways in the arid Southwest have dried up from saltcedar's hearty appetite for water.

True to its name, saltcedar contains salt in the leaves. Salts are naturally occurring in the soil. Saltcedar roots absorb these salts from the soil, transport them through the plant, and concentrate them in the leaves. These tiny, scaly leaves eventually fall off the shrub and onto the ground below. The leaves decompose and leave behind many minerals, including the salts. This process results in more salty or saline soils. Most other plants cannot tolerate these highly saline soils. The soil becomes less habitable to other plants, giving saltcedar the competitive edge.

This strategy makes saltcedar the bully of the riverways by crowding out plants that cannot tolerate the saline soils that it created. Saltcedar also reaches deep into the ground for water because of its substantial root system, therefore depleting the water supply for other plants that are not able to grow deep roots. In areas where water is limited, such as the arid Southwest, the ability to access water makes for a superior competitor in the plant world.

Saltcedar reproduces by a large number of small seeds. Small seeds can be easily blown long distances. In addition, these seeds can be viable for up to 45 days. Seeds can germinate within 24 hours of contact with water.

Saltcedar can also propagate from underground stems. This mechanism allows saltcedar to spread from stem parts that are torn apart during floods. Also, because stem and root parts can grow to become an entirely new saltcedar plant, hand-pulling alone is futile unless all root parts are retrieved.

WHAT DAMAGE DOES SALTCEDAR CAUSE?

Saltcedar consumes an enormous amount of water. Because its water consumption is so high, large stands of saltcedar have the reputation of drying up small streams. Much of this water is contained within the plant parts and then evaporates from the leaves. **Evapotranspiration** is the process whereby water evaporates from the soil and plant parts. Saltcedar has a high evapotranspiration rate, much higher than most native shrubs in the Southwest. The good news is that if a stream has dried up because of a large saltcedar infestation, removal of the stand will often allow the water to begin flowing again.

Saltcedar grows so robustly in riparian (riverbank) areas that it displaces native trees such as cottonwood, willow, and mesquite. Native birds rely on native shrubs and trees for their seeds as a food source and nest in their branches. The displacement by saltcedar causes a loss of valuable habitat and food for native wildlife since they evolved with native shrubs and trees, not introduced ones.

Saltcedar can grow so dense that animals, including people, may have a hard time physically getting to the water. Canoeists along the Colorado River are familiar with the bright pink flowers that line much of the river.

Riparian areas tend to be the most biologically rich because of the presence of water, particularly in the arid Southwest; these areas represent as little as 1% of all land. As saltcedar replaces the native cottonwood-willow riparian forest, most scientists believe we will have less bird diversity because many species are simply not able to make saltcedar their home or food source. Nature does continue to surprise us however, as scientists have discovered that an endangered species of bird, the Southwestern willow flycatcher (*Empidonax trailii extimus*), makes a home in saltcedar stands. Concern for this species has further complicated management strategies for this invasive shrub.

HOW CAN SALTCEDAR BE CONTROLLED?

Small seedlings are most easily controlled by hand-pulling, assuming all the roots are pulled out. Mature trees must be

Controlling Invasive Plants at the Local Level

Native plant societies, environmental groups, cooperative extension agencies, master gardeners, and county governments are all local groups that can help with identifying and controlling invasive plants. Whether landowners have a small garden or 10,000-acre ranch, they can enlist the help of these professionals to control their invasive plants.

In Estes Park, Colorado, home of Rocky Mountain National Park, residents feared the spread of invasive plants into the park. Local groups organized with county officials to create an Annual Weed Roundup. Residents pulled noxious weeds, placed them in bags, and brought them to a collection site for proper disposal. Each year, county officials collect hundreds of bags of various knapweeds and thistles. These bags contain hundreds of thousands of viable seeds that could spread invasive plants throughout Estes Park and Rocky Mountain National Park.

Cooperative extension agencies, as part of state universities, exist in nearly all states with local offices in every county to assist people with a range of agricultural topics. Cooperative extension Web sites provide a multitude of information on controlling specific invasive plants. Master gardeners are volunteers that are trained to answer questions about gardening and weeds, and can be reached by contacting your local cooperative extension office. Almost all county governments have a department that manages the county public lands or open space; part of this department's job is to manage invasive plant species. County governments are not only concerned with invasive plants on their properties but also on private lands. It is crucial for agencies to partner together, because although people may recognize ownership boundaries, invasive plants do not.

cut and then herbicides are applied to the root stump. The chemical in the herbicide is systemic, meaning it is able to move throughout the plant parts. In this case, the herbicide would move from the cut stump down to the roots to kill all parts of the plant, otherwise saltcedar would resprout.

In some situations, saltcedar stands are so thick that hand-pulling and root stump applications of herbicides are not practical. For these multiple-acre infestations, a bulldozer or fire is used to destroy all aboveground growth of saltcedar. The shrub resprouts and then herbicides are sprayed to the leaves. Burning is usually only advised in areas where there are no native trees growing since the fire would injure all vegetation.

What happens to this barren riparian area after being stripped of its vegetation? This is where restoration ecologists would step in to select the appropriate native species to plant. If no competitive species were planted, then saltcedar would quickly return, particularly if saltcedar has already flowered and set seed that season. In most cases, fire has to reach extremely high temperatures for viable seeds to be destroyed.

One weakness of saltcedar is that seedlings tend to grow more slowly than native plants. By planting native seedlings instead of just seeds after a saltcedar control effort such as bulldozing, fire, or spraying, native plants will have a head start on this invasive plant. Planting seedlings quickly after a burn also helps to reduce soil erosion since the root system helps prevent soil from being washed away.

Saltcedar Along the Mojave

Using fire to restore land from a saltcedar invasion was successful at the Bureau of Land Management's (BLM) Barstow Resource Area in Afton Canyon, located on the Mojave River, 38 miles northwest of Barstow, California. The main objective of removing the saltcedar was to improve wildlife habitat within the canyon bottom. Before the fire was set, photo monitoring plots were established within the stands of saltcedar that were to be burned. Photo monitoring takes a picture of the land that is being changed in some way. Just as old photographs of family members easily show how people have changed over time, the same concept applies for photo monitoring of plots that are part of a burn: The photos easily show before and after differences.

At the site, the saltcedar was so thick with heavy branches and woody material that it was difficult to access the plots. Firebreaks were set up so that the fire would not spread out of control and ignite homes. The fire was lit in July and the high temperatures, low humidity, and light wind proved ideal for the burn. Flames reached 100 feet (30 meters) tall. The intensity of the fire killed the saltcedar outright in some areas. Remember that saltcedar is a perennial so it is able to resprout; after this burn the saltcedar resprouted in one month.

The main benefit of the burn is that it clears the dense saltcedar stands so that the new sprouts can be sprayed with a herbicide. A mature saltcedar tree is not as easily controlled with herbicides and usually involves an injection of herbicide into the stump. After a year, restoration efforts began to plant willows and cottonwoods with the help of BLM staff, high school volunteers, and prison inmates. Native plants also resprouted after the fire.

As a result of this restoration effort, wildlife returned to the canyon including Say's phoebe, bobcats, bighorn sheep, coyotes, and many other birds and wildlife because of the access to water. Saltcedar is sprayed when it is found but this invasive plant will never be allowed to become the thick stand it once was because of continuous monitoring and rapid response.

Biological Control

Introducing insects that will feed on saltcedar is a form of biological control. Introducing natural predators can help replicate the natural process that keeps saltcedar in check in its native regions.

Currently there are two species of insects that scientists have learned are pests of saltcedar. One pest is a mealybug (*Trabutina mannipara*) from Israel that feeds on the twigs of saltcedar. The other pest is a leaf beetle (*Diorhabda elongate*) from China that feeds on saltcedar leaves. Some scientists believe these two insects could control 85% of saltcedar infestations. However, it is important to remember that control is not immediate. Insect populations take years to establish and to produce significant results. Using the two insects mentioned, it is estimated that it would take three to five years for control of small infestations and as much as 10 years for control of large infestations. These insects have not been released yet because of concerns for the endangered Southwestern willow flycatcher. As discussed, this bird is native but is able to use saltcedar for nesting. Natural resource managers are concerned that control of saltcedar in areas where this bird lives may further endanger it. Natural resource management is an art of balance.

The best way to prevent and manage saltcedar invasions is to maintain a healthy river system. Many natural resource managers have observed that saltcedar is much less invasive along rivers that have maintained natural processes such as periodic spring flooding. Flooding is a natural and vital process of rivers because floods bring nutrients to the lands adjacent to the water, known as the floodplain. Most native trees and shrubs benefit by having the soil around their roots supplied with mineral-rich sediment from these spring floods. Human activities such as damming of rivers have altered this flooding period from spring to summer, which tends to favor saltcedar. Other activities that favor saltcedar are increased salinity or saltiness of rivers due to irrigation and evaporation from reservoirs. Saltcedar can tolerate highly saline soil, respective to native plants; therefore it can tolerate soils that have become more saline due to irrigation technology.

Saltcedar has been in the United States for approximately 200 years and has spread to an estimated one million acres. Because this weed has been in the United States for so long, some populations of saltcedar are genetically distinct from the ones that were originally brought here. It is believed that these genetically different saltcedar trees occurred through hybridization of two or more species. In plants, hybridization is the breeding of a female plant species and a male plant from a different species. Hybridization of weed species complicates control strategies because these new species have better tolerance to the climatic conditions of the Southwest than the original species from which they derived.

Land managers realize that the eradication of saltcedar is no longer a realistic goal. When an invasive plant has been established for more than a hundred years, it is unlikely that all plant parts and seeds can be removed from all the ecosystems it has invaded. Control, however, is still possible. By identifying saltcedar when it first invades and reacting rapidly, many acres of native riparian vegetation can be preserved. In areas that have been aggressively displaced by saltcedar, a combination of burning, bulldozing, herbicides, and revegetation can make dried-up streams flow once again.

Yellow Starthistle

HORSES CHEWING
THEMSELVES TO DEATH

7

• •

Yellow starthistle (*Centaurea solstitialis*) was introduced to the United States from Eurasia accidentally as a contaminant in alfalfa seed. It began its spread in California in alfalfa stands but was quickly spread by tractors to other locations. Yellow starthistle grows on roadsides, rangeland, and pastures (Figure 7.1). Its spread was largely attributable to extensive road building, increased suburban development, and an expansion in the ranching industry. Activities such as development contribute greatly to the spread of invasive plants because construction equipment tends to move weed seeds large distances. The soil disturbance that accompanies development also provides an open environment for invasives to exploit.

People and animals can inadvertently contribute to spreading yellow starthistle. The seeds of this plant are covered with short and stiff bristles that have microscopic, hairlike barbs that can adhere to clothing, hair, and fur.

HOW DOES YELLOW STARTHISTLE AFFECT ANIMALS?

Just as the name starthistle suggests, spines protruding from the flower resemble a star. These spines are painful to cattle when eaten; therefore grazing animals will avoid lands that are heavily infested with yellow starthistle.

Figure 7.1   Yellow starthistle is poisonous to horses, causing a neurological disease referred to as chewing disease. The starlike bracts on the plant cause injury to other animals that attempt to eat it. This invasive plant has plagued rangelands primarily in California. Surrounding states are on the watch to prevent yellow starthistle from spreading to their state.

The most significant effect to animals, horses specifically, is a toxicity that causes chewing disease. Chewing disease is a neurological disorder that occurs when a horse eats yellow starthistle. Poisoning usually occurs after animals have been eating fresh or dried portions of the plant for 30 to 60 days. At first the animal will appear drowsy, have difficulty eating and drinking, and may have twitching lips and a flicking tongue. If a horse continues to feed on this plant, the animal will get abnormalities in the brain tissue (lesions) and mouth ulcers. The symptoms of yellow starthistle poisoning have been said to resemble human symptoms from Parkinson's disease. These are uncontrollable jerky movements, shaking, and muscle rigidity when at rest. Unfortunately, there is no treatment for this disease and the horses usually die from starvation and dehydration. In some cases, a farmer or rancher may not even know that he or she is feeding yellow starthistle to the horse because it has been harvested with alfalfa, baled, and sold as hay feed.

HOW DOES YELLOW STARTHISTLE COMPETE?

Yellow starthistle is an annual with seed production as high as 29,000 seeds per square meter. High seed viability is also another characteristic of starthistle seeds, with 95% of seeds being able to germinate. Although most of these seeds will germinate within the following year, some can last ten years or more in the soil. This is referred to as long seed dormancy.

Although yellow starthistle is an annual and its roots will not survive the winter, this plant still puts a tremendous amount of energy into root growth after seeds have germinated. By late spring, the roots are already 3 feet (.9 meter) long below the ground. This extensive root system enables yellow starthistle to outcompete shallow-rooted species during drier summer months when moisture is limited near the soil surface. Long

Figure 7.2 Monitoring is a crucial part of any invasive plant management program. Land managers can use monitoring equipment to know the exact location of a previous invasive plant infestation. The site would then be repeatedly evaluated to make sure the invasive plant does not come back.

after most other annual species have dried up because they generally have shorter root systems, yellow starthistle thrives in the hot and dry California sun.

Yellow starthistle also maintains its highly competitive status with spines and toxic plant parts. Spines deter all grazing animals. The toxicity to horses ensures that areas with this weed will not be heavily grazed. Animals choose to eat another plant that does not have painful spines. In addition to these mechanisms providing protection, competing plants will be consumed as the animal moves on to a more appealing plant. Grazing, often used in a weed management plan, cannot be used to control this weed.

HOW CAN YELLOW STARTHISTLE BE CONTROLLED?

Prevention is the best strategy for invasive plant species control. Once an invasive plant has invaded the area, it is crucial to get rid of it right away. If much time elapses before control begins, the plant will probably never be completely eradicated from a site. In these situations, even if all the plants are killed with chemicals or fire, usually the soil contains seeds that can germinate for the next 10 to 20 years.

The most obvious way to prevent new weed infestations is to forbid the introduction of carriers of seeds. One realistic option is certified weed-free hay, mulch, and seed. Vehicles that carry plant parts with viable seeds on the undercarriage of the car cannot be prohibited, but people can be encouraged to check under their vehicle and pluck branches off if they have been driving through yellow starthistle-infested fields. Educating people about what yellow starthistle is and how it affects the environment is a necessary part of an active campaign. In states where it has not become widespread, land management agencies post signs with a picture of the weed and what it does, alerting the hiker, fisherman, or hunter to call a staff member if they come across it.

Another component of any prevention campaign is to determine high-risk areas for new infestations and regularly monitor those lands. Scientists know that yellow starthistle favors high light intensity locations such as south-facing slopes and disturbed sites, particularly roadsides. Sites with those characteristics and close proximity to yellow starthistle sites should be checked regularly by land managers (Figure 7.2). In the event that a new population is discovered, an aggressive campaign to eradicate the weed will likely remove it from the site.

Figure 7.3 Most of the world uses mechanical methods of control to remove unwanted plants. Mechanical control includes hoeing, hand-pulling, tillage, and mowing. The disadvantage of mechanical control is that resprouting is common for plants that reproduce from root pieces.

Mechanical Control

High seed production suggests that the first step in controlling this plant is preventing additional seed production. Hand-pulling, hoeing, tillage, or mowing will cut the portion of the plant that contains the seeds or flowers (Figure 7.3). The problem, however, is that even though yellow starthistle is an annual, the roots can resprout. Land managers must make sure that if tillage is used, the soil is dry, otherwise fragmented plant parts will take advantage of the moisture to resprout. If roots are separated from shoots, then the plant parts of the yellow starthistle will not create a new plant. Similarly, people oftentimes will take a cutting from a houseplant to start their own. When they do, they make sure to include a shoot—this is where the plant branches off from the stem. The root cannot propagate on its own without the shoot.

Biological Control

Three weevils (*Bangasternus orientalis*, *Eustenopus villosus*, and *Larinus curtus*) and a gall fly (*Urophora sirunaseua*) have been imported from Greece and established as predators of yellow starthistle in California. They all attack the flower or seed head depending on what phase the weed is in. The insects lay their eggs in, on, or near the flower or seed heads to complete the development of the insect eggs to larvae and then adult. This process is stressful to yellow starthistle and reduces its seed production, which is the primary form of reproduction for this plant. The insects are host-specific, meaning that they attack only their host, yellow starthistle, and do not attack any other valuable plant, particularly crops.

The benefit of biological control is that it implements a self-sustaining system. Land managers do not have to go back every season to release new insects. The initial insects that are released may only survive the season but they will lay new eggs

Herbicide Resistance

Plants adapt to their environment; they are able to change genetically to be more competitive in their environment. Given this, it makes sense that developing resistance to these synthetic compounds created to kill them would make them more competitive. Herbicide resistance is when a weed becomes tolerant to a chemical to which it was previously susceptible. Amazingly, developing this resistance often takes only a few years.

Herbicide resistance develops when just a few plants alter and become resistant to the chemical. The resistant plants may be small in number initially, but these plants will be the ones whose genes are passed on through reproduction. The new population will have the genes for resistance and the newly resistant weeds will quickly replace the susceptible plants.

Herbicides kill plants through a few different mechanisms, referred to as modes of action. Mode of action refers to the sequence of events from the moment the herbicide is absorbed into the plant until the plant's death. Some herbicides inhibit photosynthesis, which causes the plant to starve. Another mode of action classification is growth regulators. Growth regulators cause plant growth abnormalities that eventually lead to death.

Triazine is a chemical compound that weeds such as kochia (*Kochia scoparia*) are resistant to. The mode of action for triazine is

for the next season. And since each insect lays many eggs and potentially each of those eggs becomes an adult that lays many eggs, the population will increase exponentially. Generally, it does take a few years after the initial release of insects for a notable reduction in yellow starthistle. Activities that cause inhibiting photosynthesis. Photosynthesis inhibitors shut down the photosynthetic (food-producing) process in susceptible plants by binding to specific sites within the plant's chloroplasts. Triazine-resistant plants are able to continue normal photosynthesis upon exposure to triazine because of a slight change in a chloroplast protein.*

Corn has a different strategy for avoiding the photosynthesis-inhibiting effects of triazine. Corn quickly deactivates triazine by binding it to naturally occurring plant chemicals.**

To cope with these challenges, herbicide users such as farmers, ranchers, and natural resource managers have developed a few tricks to outsmart these ever-changing plants. One strategy to prevent herbicide resistance is to vary the kinds of herbicides that are used. In addition, an herbicide with a different mode of action can be used. Another strategy is to use a different method of weed control such as mechanical means or crop rotation. Crop rotation is altering the years that a specific crop is planted. Certain weeds tend to associate with particular crops, so rotating crops will help to confuse weeds and other pests.

*Jeffrey L. Gunsolus and William C. Curran. *Herbicide Mode of Action and Injury Symptoms.* University of Minnesota. North Central Regional Publication 377.

**Ibid.

heavy disturbance such as soil cultivation should be suspended for a few years until the insects get a chance to establish their populations.

Another advantage of biological control perceived by land managers is its popularity with the public. Although there are potential dangers to the environment of introducing nonnative insects, most landowners prefer their use instead of herbicides. Releasing insects to control weeds is perceived as more environmentally friendly and less likely to generate opposition for use on public lands.

Figure 7.4 Spraying herbicides is also referred to as a method of chemical plant control. Herbicides are generally quite effective but public concern is high when using them on public lands. Land managers must take precautions to prevent injury to native plants or pollution of water sources.

Chemical Control

Herbicides are a common tool for controlling invasive plant species and are generally the easiest and cheapest form of control (Figure 7.4). Results are immediate but usually have to be repeated each season. Many farmers and ranchers use herbicides regularly to maintain their property.

Many products are labeled for yellow starthistle control. Applicators must be very careful about using them near water (unless it is an aquatic herbicide) or near endangered plant species. Drift to neighboring properties is also a concern. Applicators must ensure that accurate records are maintained. The majority of the public is very concerned about the use of synthetic (artificially manufactured rather than natural) herbicides and therefore, land managers must use good judgment when deciding upon their use.

Figure 7.5 Although barren land will naturally revegetate over time, most land managers choose to plant seeds of desirable plants to help establish a healthy plant community more quickly. A healthy plant community will help prevent invasive plants from returning.

REVEGETATION

Once the yellow starthistle is controlled, it is important to replace bare ground with desirable vegetation. If left bare, invasive species will return to the land. **Revegetation** is the process of putting back desirable plants with either seeds, seedlings, or mature plants (Figure 7.5). Species chosen should be based on the desirable use for the land and species that are known to be competitive to the weed. Quick-growing grass species tend to be competitive to yellow starthistle; perennial bunch grasses tend to grow more slowly and therefore have moderate success.

Even with the best efforts to control invasive plant species from the area, viable seeds will be left in the seed bank that can germinate and become new invasive plants. Revegetation aims to seed with enough desirable plants that the starthistle seeds that germinate will not dominate the landscape once again. Unfortunately, there is no way to kill ungerminated weed seeds, with the exception of an extremely high-temperature fire; however, the temperature required would also damage the soil.

Fighting With Fire

8

Fire has been used to maintain the health of the environment since the time of the early Native Americans. The Blackfoot Indians were named because of the prairie fire ash on their feet. As devastating as the aftereffect of a fire may appear, it is an integral part of natural resource management.

PRESCRIBED BURNING

Fire that is intentionally set to benefit the land is referred to as prescribed burning. For nearly 100 years, agencies like the U.S. Forest Service regularly suppressed fires. After much research, land managers discovered that the key to a healthy forest includes burns. Now land management agencies include prescribed burns in their management plans.

Fire and Wildlife Habitat

Prescribed burning is often used to improve wildlife habitat. Fire improves wildlife habitat by increasing wildlife food sources and changing vegetation structure. Depending on the direction that the land faces (north, south, east, or west), newly burned areas tend to green up sooner in the spring allowing wildlife species longer periods of highly nutritious food as animals move from sprouted burned areas to newly sprouting unburned areas.

Burns are used to change plant species, removing the dominance of a less-favorable plant species on a site for one more favorable for food. A burn may be initiated to remove sagebrush from a site to increase grass and broadleaf plant production. Some animals, especially birds, need structures that either provide hiding cover or allow them to see over long distances. Perennial shrubs, after they are burned, increase the number of shoots and thus create cover for small mammals or songbirds. The mountain plover, a bird unique to short-grass prairies, requires short grasses for nesting, because its main escape mechanism is sighting predators over long distances. When grazing is not available, burning can be used to produce the grass stand structure necessary for the plover.

One of the biggest threats in using prescribed fire for wildlife habitat is removing cover that may be inhibiting the proliferation of nonnative plants. In Colorado, prescribed fire was used to improve bighorn sheep habitat. However, when the overstory of sagebrush was removed, smooth bromegrass (*Bromus tectorum*), commonly know as cheatgrass, completely took over the site. It is assumed, since most nonnatives create large, tenacious seed sources, that dormant seeds on the ground germinated when the site became more favorable after the fire. Therefore, when prescribed fire is used to promote wildlife habitat, it is important to immediately treat the area to prohibit nonnative plant growth. Reseeding with natives or cultivation or any other effort that prohibits nonnative growth can reduce the threat of invasive species invasions.[6]

Preventing Wildfires

Ignite a fire to prevent one? This may seem odd but prescribed burning can prevent out-of-control wildfires. Forests accumulate needles, branches, and other natural debris on the forest floor. Fire will clear not only the forest floor of these ground fuels, but will induce "limbing up," or burning off the lower branches of pines that will eventually die and fall off. The tree will no longer have to expend energy on these lower branches and the result is a higher crown height for the tree. A higher crown height and fewer lower limbs also makes the tree more fire resistant.

Another benefit of prescribed burning is that in the event of a wildland fire from lightning, arson, or human carelessness, the intensity of the fire is decreased. The ground fuels are removed from the prescribed burn, so in the event that another fire takes place, it will be less likely to grow to an unmanageable fire. Prescribed burns are much smaller than the out-of-control forest fires you hear about in the media.

Fires also increase grass and broadleaf plants that are of particular importance to grazing and woodland animals. By burning a portion of the forest, there is more diversity in habitat because there will still be forest but also some clearings with grass species. Burning different areas at different intervals and seasons produces a diversity of landscapes, animal food, and cover sources. Burning also promotes seed germination, flowering, or resprouting of fire-adapted native plants, thus increasing availability of nuts and fruits for wildlife. Prescribed fire intervals of two to four years are generally used to promote this diversity.

Many people add fertilizer to their lawn to increase the soil fertility, which will provide more nutrients for the plants. The result is a greener and lusher lawn. Nature has its own way of fertilizing the land. Fire returns nutrients to the soil from the burned plants. New sprouts capture the quick flush of nutrients into the soil after a fire and are often more nutritious than older plants.

FIRE AND INVASIVE TERRESTRIAL PLANTS

Invasive plants can spread so aggressively that they can completely take over a landscape where no other plant species grow. Usually this is a situation where the weed problem went either unnoticed or unmanaged for years. Weed management at this stage is extremely difficult because of the depth of perennial roots and number of viable seeds in the soil and above.

Fire can be used to remove the aboveground portion of the plant. Even in an extremely hot fire, the roots will remain undamaged; therefore if the invasive plant is a perennial, the roots will likely resprout. It is still advantageous to use fire for perennials. Oftentimes the weed has grown so thick that physical access can be difficult. In some cases, heavy equipment is the only thing that can remove a monoculture for an invasive such as saltcedar. Another concern is physical injury if the plant has prickly parts such as Canada thistle. Plants such as spotted and diffuse knapweed can be difficult to remove because of the hives they cause on some people.

Fire is a way to remove difficult plants. It is also a tool to use in areas near water. Herbicides are generally used when an area has been aggressively taken over by invasive plants; however, some lands are too close to water. Sandy soils are also a concern when applying herbicides. Sandy soils are more porous, allowing for more passage by liquid. Herbicides sprayed on a sandy soil could more easily enter the groundwater if it is not too far below the soil surface. Sandy soils and proximity to water preclude the use of many herbicides. In these cases, fire is a practical tool.

Fire is also used by farmers to free irrigation ditches of thick vegetation that slows water flow. Removing the weeds is additionally critical because their rapid growth consumes valuable water that is intended for irrigation.

After the Fire

Fires expose ground surfaces, reduce shade, and create a flush of soil nutrients—conditions that favor the establishment of noxious weeds. Given the preceding statement, it may seem odd to use fire to *control* weeds when fire creates conditions that favor weeds. An instrumental part of using fire to control weeds is to revegetate or reseed after the fire. Newly revegetated seedlings or mature plants will capture this flush of nutrients and compete with any weeds that either travel to the site or germinate from viable seeds still left in the soil.

If the land is to be seeded, an aggressive, quick-growing mix of grasses and broadleaf plants is most competitive with weeds. Of particular concern should be areas that are sloped or the proximity of drainage because both of these are more likely to have soil erosion unless vegetation is quickly established.

If you have ever planted flowers in a garden, the soil had to be dug, the plant inserted, and then the soil placed appropriately around the plant. Similarly, when revegetating a landscape, the seedbed must be prepared. Seedbed preparation refers to any modifications one would make to the soil before seeding. Seedbed preparation may include tillage to break up compacted dirt so that seedlings can easily thrust their roots into the depth of the soil as they grow.

When burned areas are reseeded during the fall after a fire, they usually do not require seedbed preparation. Ash from the fire helps cover and retain broadcasted seeds. Have you ever noticed the number of potholes that appear after a series of icy or snowy days mixed with a few warmer ones? The potholes are a result of water expanding as it freezes. The frozen water expands in the tiny cracks in the road, further breaking apart the asphalt. When the water thaws, the potholes appear. The wet and dry, freeze and thaw action of moisture is beneficial in preparing the seedbed. This process will work the seeds into the soil while also breaking down soil layers that tend to clump. Frost heaving, an upthrust of the soil caused by freezing of moist soil, will break down ash crusts that form because of fall rains.

Increasing the seeding rate will also help the desirable species be more competitive because there will be more of them.

If the ash layer is not substantial, a seedbed can be prepared by dragging small chains or raking the soil surface before and after seeding.[7] If the seedbed is not prepared, a smaller percentage of the seeds will germinate.

Choosing the Right Plants

The first priority is that the plants used to revegetate should be competitive to the weed that was there. Even if the weed was an annual with roots that do not resprout and the burn was thorough, the weeds will be back, just to a lesser extent. Weeds return because there are viable seeds in the soil that the fire could not destroy.

Plants that are adapted to the site will generally have the best chance of thriving long-term. Native species are an obvious choice; however, cultivars are also a good option. A cultivar is a cultivated variety. In some cases a plant is genetically altered to "improve" a plant. Many of the roses available in nurseries are cultivars. A common rose cultivar is the hybrid tea rose. This plant has been modified so that it is almost always blooming during the growing season.

Cultivars can also be plants that are vegetatively propagated, otherwise known as clones. Clones would be cultivated because the plant is seen as desirable. Hybrids can also be cultivars. Once established, they produce seeds that can become new plants; they are fertile, which is significant considering that many hybrids are sterile.

It is important to select plants that occupy different niches. A niche is a plant's role in the ecological community. A shallow-rooted plant consumes water in the upper layers of the soil. A deep-rooted plant acquires water far below the soil surface. A healthy community has plants that get water and nutrients from varying depths of the soil profile. By filling up all of the niches, there is less availability for an invader species to fill in.

Choosing the Right Weed Management Strategy

The next step in the revegetation process is to decide which weed management techniques should be used. For the first year of establishment of desirable plants, mowing is likely to be the only feasible method of control. Most herbicides for use on noncrop plants require that the plants are well established with a secondary root system (more than just the taproot) and tillering (side shoots) for grasses.

Mowing before seeds are formed is adequate control of annual weeds but is not sufficient for perennials. Generally the mower blade is set high to cut the taller weeds but not cut the shorter, slower-growing plants. Land managers mow the weeds when they are two to three times higher than the grasses. Also, the land is not mowed any closer than 8 to 12 inches (20 to 30 centimeters) above the ground. This may seem strange when you think of how short lawns and turf are cut; however, in restoration, land managers want grasses to flower and produce valuable seeds that can germinate and crowd out incoming weeds. Cutting grasses too short will prevent them from being able to flower and seed.

Monitoring is also important once the vegetation is established and the initial weed management has been implemented. Sites should be periodically inspected and mapped if any initial weed populations show up. This last step may seem tedious but if monitoring and early detection along with a rapid response were used originally, the land would not have needed to be restored.

9 The Future of Plants

• •

Invasive terrestrial plants will continue to be an environmental issue even if all travel were to cease. Most efforts consist of stemming the tide of invasives that have invaded previously pristine lands. As our understanding and capabilities sharpen, we should be able to accomplish more than just maintaining existing acreages of invasive species.

Native species are at risk of being outcompeted by invasive plants. Plants already at risk, endangered and threatened species, are being pushed closer to extinction. Habitat loss and overexploitation have been the primary human-induced causes of species extinction. Habitat loss includes destruction of rain forests and wetlands. **Overexploitation** is using a species for food, clothing, or some other purpose to the point of overuse and subsequent extinction. Today, introduction of invasive species, including plants, is being cited as a primary reason for species extinctions.

PUSHING ENDANGERED SPECIES TO EXTINCTION

All plant species have a function in the ecosystem. Scientists are still not aware of all the species that exist and what their roles are. Malaysia has about 12,000 species of flowering plants of which about 1,300 are said to be medicinal, and only about 100 have been investigated.[8] In addition to each of these plants having a value in the ecosystem, many of them can be developed for use as medicines. If we lose these plants before we have a chance to find out, we will never know what riches we have lost.

Without terrestrial plants, the Earth would be a barren place since animals and insects rely on plants for food and shelter. It is devastating to lose even one species of plant. Due to the disruptive nature of invasive plant species, threatened and endangered plant species have been pushed closer to extinction.

SELECTIVE MANAGEMENT

In Iowa, the northern wild monkshood (*Aconitum noveboracense*) is on the federal endangered and threatened species list. Monkshood is a perennial that lives in the pastures of Iowa (Figure 9.1). Unfortunately these same pastures are being invaded by Canada thistle and other pasture weeds. Land managers face a challenge to control these weeds without killing the threatened monkshood. The best strategy is to eradicate the weeds before they have invaded the same habitat as the monkshood. If the weeds and monkshood have already overlapped, control is extremely difficult since mowing would injure both plants, as would herbicides. Most herbicides for use in pastures kill all broadleaf species and do not harm grasses; this is an example of a selective herbicide. Nonselective herbicides kill both broadleaf and grass plants. If no control strategy is implemented, then the Canada thistle will completely dominate the pasture and the monkshood will be outcompeted, probably never to return to that site again unless an aggressive restoration project is implemented.

Another option is to use wiper technology. Just as the name indicates, weeds are "wiped" with herbicides so that desirable plants such as the monkshood are not accidentally injured. The wiper tool is shaped like a hockey stick with a spongelike material at the bottom. The applicator walks around the

Figure 9.1   Many rare plant species such as monkshood are threatened by invasive species. Invasive species are now considered one of the biggest threats, along with habitat loss, to threatened and endangered species.

pasture and dabs each weed with the wiper, which contains an herbicide. Wiper technology is tedious but it ensures that endangered and threatened species are not accidentally injured or killed.

INVASIVE PLANTS AND POLICY

According to Cornell University, invasive plants cost the United States $35.5 billion annually. Invasive plants displace native plants, reduce biodiversity, affect threatened and endangered species, decrease wildlife habitat, and reduce recreational value. Many of these factors cannot be translated into monetary losses. As a result, governmental as well as nongovernmental agencies have successfully lobbied for regulations to control the influx of invasive plants.

Laws exist at both the federal and state levels to control invasive plants and their seeds. In 1999, the federal government created the National Invasive Species Council comprised of federal employees to coordinate effective federal activities regarding invasive species. In 2001, the council released the National Invasive Species Management Plan and the council is currently setting up task teams and subcommittees to implement the action items of the plan. One aspect of this plan is education and public awareness. The control of invasive species will require modifying behaviors, values, and beliefs and changing the way decisions are made regarding our actions. The council suggests in their plan such outreach activities as a national public awareness campaign as well as an international education campaign, because, as mentioned, invasive species know no boundaries.

States are entitled to have their own regulations for invasive plant control. Many of the western states have stricter invasive plant or weed laws because their economies rely more on agriculture. The state of Colorado has a state list of noxious

Using Dogs to Detect Invasive Plants

Dogs have a heightened sense of smell. They have been trained to detect drugs, bombs, and even prohibited agricultural products. Now they are being trained to detect invasive plants.

Using dogs to find invasive plants was initiated in Montana with efforts specifically focused on spotted knapweed. Spotted knapweed costs Montana $42 million per year in control and forage loss. "Knapweed Nightmare" is the name of a Rocky Mountain shepherd, the first dog being trained for the purpose of detecting spotted knapweed.

Dogs are trained to focus on a certain scent and therefore would have more success in detecting spotted knapweed or other invasive plants early and alerting land managers to their exact location. Currently the only way new infestations are discovered is usually accidental because most ranchers and farmers do not have the time or resources to fan out over their acreages searching for new weeds.

Dogs are trained to the scent of a specific weed by bundling plant samples in towels to create toys for the dog to find. Once the dog has mastered that task, hiding places get more difficult and eventually toys are tucked in a larger area amid other smells.

The challenge is setting the dog free on expansive rangeland with the distractions of wildlife. A dog's success will be monitored using a Global Positioning System (GPS) mounted on the dog's collar. GPS equipment collects electronic data from satellites that pinpoint the location. GPS data is usually downloaded to a map showing the geographically referenced locations. Once the dog has found spotted knapweed, it will scratch and dig for about 10 seconds. The GPS monitor is set up to track her location every three seconds. If the dog is found to have paused at a particular location, that site will be inspected for spotted knapweed.

weeds. In Colorado, it is illegal to grow or plant any of the plants on the list. Enforcement occurs at the county level and most Colorado counties additionally restrict plants they perceive as troublesome. In Larimer County, Colorado, county employees regularly monitor landowner properties by driving through streets and alleys and looking for noxious weeds. Personnel are trained to identify weeds. Properties with noxious weeds are recorded and a letter is sent to the landowner requesting the removal of the weed. In the worst-case scenario of noncompliance, county officials may enter onto the land and mow the weeds. The property would be assessed a tax to encourage compliance in subsequent years.

The Connecticut Department of Environmental Protection (DEP) has a nonnative invasive plant species policy to curb and control expansion and introduction of nonnative species in Connecticut. The policy prohibits the intentional planting or introduction of invasive plants on DEP lands, recommends the preparation and distribution of educational materials to the public on the invasive species issue, and encourages invasive plants to be controlled on both public and private lands. Most states have adopted similar policies.

LOOKING TOWARD TOMORROW

Geographic barriers are being removed as travel and access increase in the creation of a more integrated, globalized society (Figure 9.2). Since plants travel primarily through the actions of people, geographic barriers to plants also are being removed. The removal of these barriers tends to be at the expense of native plants with narrow ecological roles.

Travel will continue and so will the opportunity for additional invaders. Without intervention, the world could be filled with nothing but wide-niche, generalist species, once considered invasive but occupying lands for so long that

Figure 9.2 Global trade is one of the main ways invasive species, including plants, have been able to get around the globe so quickly. Invasive species often travel in the ballast water or among cargo.

they are considered part of the natural landscape. If creative solutions such as training dogs to locate plants are used along with the reliable methods of tillage, mowing, and crop rotation, we may be able to preserve the integrity and uniqueness of our ecosystems. Governmental policy is the vehicle for change. As scientists and policymakers work together to formulate the best plan to control invasive terrestrial plants, we can continue to live in a world of ecological richness, with plants living in the place where nature intended.

NOTES

1. John M. Randall and Janet Marinelli. *Invasive Plants: Weeds of the Global Garden.* Brooklyn, NY: Brooklyn Botanic Gardens, 1996, p. 13.

2. Toby and Will Musgrave. *An Empire of Plants.* London: Cassell and Company, 2000, p.65.

3. Anthony Huxley, *Green Inheritance. The World Wildlife Fund Book of Plants.* New York: Doubleday, 1985, pp. 11–23, 91, 115.

4. Ibid.

5. Sonia DiFiore. *Introduced Species Summary Project Small Indian Mongoose* (*Herpestes auropunctatus*). New York: Columbia University, 2000.

6. John R. Bustos, Jr., USDA Forest Service, Public Affairs Officer, Arapaho and Roosevelt National Forests and Pawnee National Grassland, Personal Communication, 2005.

7. Roger L. Sheley. *Invasive Plant Management: CIPM Online Textbook.* USDA/ARS. Available online at: http://www.weedcenter.org/textbook.

8. Nutrition Society of Malaysia. Biotechnology and Natural Products. Review of Biodiversity and Environmental Conservation. Kuala Lumpur, Malaysia. Available online at: http://www.arbec.com.my/biotech.htm.

GLOSSARY

Adaptations Small changes a plant makes over time to better compete in its environment.

Allelopathy The process by which plants are able to produce chemicals and exude them from the roots to inhibit the growth of competing species.

Annuals Plants that complete their life cycle in one growing season.

Biennials Plants that complete their life cycle in two growing seasons.

Boreal forests or taiga Biological communities comprised mostly of evergreens, with low temperatures and nutrient-poor soils; found in the broad belt of Eurasia and North America.

Botany The study of plants.

Cuticle The waterproof, outermost layer of cells on a plant that helps prevent water loss from leaves.

Entomology The study of insects.

Evapotranspiration The process whereby water evaporates from plant parts.

Exploitative competition When plants obtain resources more efficiently and rapidly than other species.

Fallowlands Previously farmed croplands that are being given a break from planting for at least one season.

Groundwater The water that flows below the soil surface, known as the zone of saturation.

Host range The kinds of plants an insect will eat.

Interference A competitive strategy where plants use antagonistic or fighting behavior such as chemicals to exclude species from an area.

Interspecific competition Competition between members of different species.

Intraspecific competition Competition between members of the same species.

Invasive terrestrial plants Exotic, highly competitive plants that do harm to our ecosystem.

Monocultures Fields of only one plant species.

Mutualistic relationship When both species benefit from an interaction.

Niche The ecological role of a species in its community.

Overexploitation Using a species for food, clothing, or some other purpose to the point of overuse and subsequent extinction.

Overwinter The period of dormancy for plants or insect larvae, usually during the winter. The organism is still alive, just not actively growing.

Pastures Grazing lands that have an improvement on the land such as fencing.

Perennials Plants that complete their life cycle in two or more years.

Plant pathology The study of plant disease.

Rangelands Grasslands, often home to grazing animals, most common in the western United States.

Revegetation The process of putting back desirable plants with either seeds, seedlings, or mature plants.

Rhizomes Also called "creeping roots." Modified stems that extend laterally underground. They usually form an extensive underground network, usually many feet deep.

Soil stabilizers Plants that fight erosion because they have extensive root systems that grab on to the soil.

Taproot The main part of the root below the ground that supports the plant and provides considerable food storage.

Terrestrial plants Woody or herbaceous plants that grow on land and use sunlight, carbon dioxide, and water to make food. Terrestrial plants get their nutrients from the soil.

Tillage Using plows or discs to cut up and bury plant parts.

BIBLIOGRAPHY

Australian Weeds Committee. *Weed Identification: Black Willow (Salix nigra)*. 2000. Available online at: http://www.weeds.org.au.

Australian Weeds Committee. *Weed Identification: Box Elder (Acer negundo)*. 2000. Available online at: http://www.weeds.org.au.

Beck, K.G. *Biology and Management of the Toadflaxes*. Colorado State University Cooperative Extension: 2000. Available online at: http://www.ext.colostate.edu/pubs/natres.

Beck, K.G. *Diffuse and Spotted Knapweed*. Colorado State University Cooperative Extension: 2000. Available online at: http://www.ext.colostate.edu/pubs/natres.

Beck, K.G. *Leafy Spurge*. Colorado State University Cooperative Extension: 2000. Available online at: http://www.ext.colostate.edu/pubs/natres.

Beck, K.G. *Musk Thistle*. Colorado State University Cooperative Extension: 2000. Available online at: http://www.ext.colostate.edu/pubs/natres.

Bustos, John R., Jr., USDA Forest Service, Public Affairs Officer, Arapaho and Roosevelt National Forests and Pawnee National Grassland. Personal Communication, 2005.

Cornell University. "Alien Animals, Plants and Microbes Cost U.S. $123 Billion a Year." 1999. Available online at: http://www.news.cornell.edu.

DiFiore, Sonia. *Introduced Species Summary Project Small Indian Mongoose (Herpestes auropunctatus)*. New York: Columbia University, 2000.

DiTomaso, Joseph. *Yellow Starthistle*. Davis: University of California Weed Research and Information Center, 2001.

Gunsolus, Jeffrey L., and William S. Curran. *Herbicide Mode of Action and Injury Symptoms.* University of Minnesota: North Central Regional Publication 377.

Horvath, Gaspar. *Windbreak Research at Iowa State University.* 2000. Available online at: http://www.forestry.iastate.edu/res/ Shelterbelt.html.

Huxley, Anthony. *Green Inheritance. The World Wildlife Fund Book of Plants.* New York: Doubleday, 1985.

Jeffrey, C. *An Introduction to Plant Taxonomy*, Second Edition. Cambridge, England: University Press, 1992.

Lym, Rodney G., and Richard K. Zollinger. *Spotted Knapweed* (*Centaurea maculosa*). Fargo: North Dakota State University, 2000.

Musgrave, Toby and Will. *An Empire of Plants.* London: Cassell and Company, 2000.

Nutrition Society of Malaysia. *Biotechnology and Natural Products. Review of Biodiversity and Environmental Conservation.* Kuala Lumpur, Malaysia. Available online at: http://www.arbec.com. my/biotech.htm.

Peterson, Dallas. *Weeds Become Resistant to Herbicides.* Fargo: North Dakota State University, 1988.

Pullen, Stephanie. *The Biomes.* University of California, Berkeley, 1996. Available online at: http://www.ucmp.berkeley.edu/ glossary/gloss5/biome.

Randall, John M., and Janet Marinelli. *Invasive Plants: Weeds of the Global Garden.* Brooklyn, N.Y.: Brooklyn Botanic Gardens, 1996.

Sheley, Roger L., Tony J. Svejcar, Bruce D. Maxwell, and James S. Jacobs. *Healthy Plant Communities.* Twin Bridges, Mont.: Montana Weed Control Association, 2000.

Sheley, Roger L. *Invasive Plant Management: CIPM Online Textbook.* USDA/ARS. 2000. Available online at: http://www.weedcenter. org/textbook.

Sheley, Roger L., Kim Goodwin, and Janet Clark. *Weed Management After Fire.* 2000. Available online at: http://www.weedcenter.org/textbook/7_fire_sheley_etal.html.

Taylor, Suzi. *Knapweed-Sniffing Dog Joins the War on Weeds.* Bozeman: Montana State University News, 2000.

U.S. Environmental Protection Agency. *Registering Pesticides,* 2000. Available online at: http://www.epa.gov/pesticides/regulating/registering.

Von Willert, Prof. Dr. Dieter J. *Ecophysiology and Ethnobotany.* Institute of Plant Ecology. University of Munster, Germany, 2000. Available online at: http://www.uni-muenster.de/Biologie.Pflanzenoekologie.

West, Bruce R. *Prescribed Burning and Wildfire (Fire as a Tool in Saltcedar Management).* U.S. Department of the Interior Bureau of Land Management, 2000.

Wilkins, Malcolm. *Plant Watching.* New York: Facts On File Publications, 1988.

FURTHER READING

Baskin, Y. *A Plague of Rats and Rubbervines: The Growing Threat of Species Invasions*. Covelo, Calif.: Shearwater Books, 2003.

Coombs, E.M., J.K. Clark, G.L. Piper, and A.F. Cofrancesco, Jr. *Biological Control of Invasive Plants in the United States*. Corvallis: Oregon State University Press, 2004.

Cox, G. *Alien Species and Evolution: The Evolutionary Ecology of Exotic Plants, Animals, Microbes, and Interacting Native Species*. Washington, D.C.: Island Press, 2004.

DiTomaso, J.M. *Aquatic and Riparian Weeds of the West*. Collingdale, Pa.: DIANE Publishing Company, 2003.

Mooney, H.A. *Invasive Species in a Changing World*. Washington, D.C.: Island Press, 2000.

Sheley, R.L. *Biology and Management of Noxious Rangeland Weeds*. Corvallis: Oregon State University Press, 1999.

Witson, T. *Weeds of the West*, Ninth Edition. Collingdale, Pa: DIANE Publishing Company, 2000.

Zimdahl, R. *Fundamentals of Weed Science*, Second Edition. New York: Academic Press, 1998.

WEB SITES

California Invasive Plant Council (Cal-IPC)
http://www.cal-ipc.org

Cornell University—Biological Control
http://www.nysaes.cornell.edu/ent/biocontrol/info/biocont.html

The Global Invasive Species Database
http://www.issg.org/database/welcome

Larimer County Weed District
http://www.larimer.org/weeds.

Minnesota Department of Natural Resources—
Invasive Terrestrial Plants
http://www.dnr.state.mn.us/invasives/terrestrialplants/index.html

The Nature Conservancy (TNC)—Invasive Plants
http://www.nature.org/initiatives/invasivespecies

University of Florida—Non-native Invasive Terrestrial
Plants in the United States
http://aquat1.ifas.ufl.edu/terinv.html

USDA Animal and Plant Health Inspection Service (APHIS)
http://www.aphis.usda.gov/ppq/weeds

USDA Forest Service Intermountain Region—Noxious Weeds
http://www.fs.fed.us/r4/resources/noxious_weeds/index.shtml

USDA Natural Resources Conservation Service
http://plants.nrcs.usda.gov/cgi_bin/topics.cgi?earl=noxious.cgi

PICTURE CREDITS

page:

12: Wally Eberhart/Visuals Unlimited
14: Peggy Greb/USDA
20: Ron Goulet/Dembinsky Photo Associates
21: Walt Anderson/Visuals Unlimited
28: Courtesy Richard Old/1,000 Weeds of North America,
    An Identification Guide, on CD ROM: www.xidservices. com
38: Courtesy Richard Old/1,000 Weeds of North America,
    An Identification Guide, on CD ROM: www.xidservices. com
39: Adam Jones/Dembinsky Photo Associates
46: Bob Richard APHIS/USDA
48: Bill Lea/Dembinsky Photo Associates
51: Joe Sroka/Dembinsky Photo Associates
53: James Young/USDA
61: Jack Dykinga/USDA
70: Stephen Ausmus/USDA
72: Scott Bauer/USDA
74: Norris Blake/Visuals Unlimited
78: Stephen Ausmus/USDA
79: Jim Hughes/Visuals Unlimited
90: Kevin & Betty Collins/Visuals Unlimited
94: David R. Frazier/Photo Researchers, Inc.

Cover: Dennis Flaherty/Photo Researchers, Inc.

INDEX

ABOUT THE AUTHOR

Suellen May writes for agricultural and environmental publications. She is a graduate of the University of Vermont (B.S.) and Colorado State University (M.S.). She has worked in the environmental field for 15 years, including invasive species management for Larimer County Parks and Open Lands in Colorado. She served as the education committee chairperson for the Colorado Weed Management Association. While living in Fort Collins, Colorado, she founded the Old Town Writers' Group, which continues to thrive. She lives with her son, Nate, in Bucks County, Pennsylvania. Readers can reach her at suellen0829@yahoo.com.